Young Sisters

A collection of experiences celebrating
the lives of teenage girls

Anna Leung

Young Sisters

Credits
Author Photo: Curtis Willocks
Cover Design: Sean Glumace and Anna Leung
Cover Design Input: Sarah Grace Seehafer
Typesetting and Interior Design: Nicki Jean Murray and Tracy Taylor
Photographs: Anna Leung

To Curtis Willocks
Thank you for everything!
Thanks for being an excellent friend, mentor, and father figure to me.

Acknowledgements

Those who have supported me with encouragement, assistance, and love to make *Young Sisters* possible are many: God, the girls who invited you and me into their lives, my photography teacher, Curtis Willocks, my mentors, Liz Skoler and June Kung. Talent Unlimited (TU) High School family: Drama class of 2001, teachers, friends, and staff; especially, Christina Glover, Flonia Telegrafi, Valerie Williams, Grace Pelosi, and George Ryan. My awesome travel partner and husband, Sam Graham. My editors Stephanie Buckwalter, Susan and Geoffrey Graham, Melanie Lo, Andrew Perry, Liz Skoler, Laurie Snyder, and Flonia Telegrafi. My fantastic sidekicks for putting the book together Sean Glumace, Sarah Grace Seehafer, Tracy Taylor, and Nicki Jean Murray. I whole-heartedly thank you all so much for everything you have contributed.

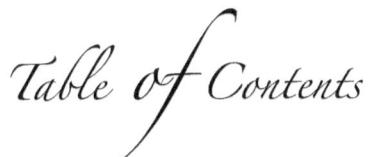

Table of Contents

None of us can change our yesterdays,
but all of us can change our tomorrows.

Colin Powell
Secretary of state of the United States of America
under President George W. Bush

Introduction

During my teenage years, I was the wildest Chinese firecracker among my peers. I was always involved with activities and embraced new opportunities that were available to me. My schedule was always full. The routine for my weekdays after school was volunteering in my community, attending after school programs or going to different lessons such as piano or karate or dance or... well, you get the point. Saturdays were dedicated to Chinese school and Sundays were devoted to church or interning for a photography professor by teaching college and adult students *Photo 101*. This was the norm for me. Everyday was unique with its own spice to it. I was young, energetic, excited to learn, loved meeting new people, willing to experiment, and the only thing that stop me from doing more was a 7 p.m. curfew.

Photography was the only activity I could not get enough of; it changed my life. I still remember what a phenomenal experience it was to be in the darkroom, to walk into a smelly "rat poison" room where films were developed and images were produced. This place was where all the magic happened. I would mix chemicals together in order to create perfect formulas needed to transfer negatives to prints. Meticulously, I agitated the developer tray at a constant tempo while my heart beat with anticipation and excitement as the image slowly revealed itself. To this day, I still remember how much my lungs hurt after coming out from the darkroom. I was so addicted to what I was doing that I refused to take a break from the fumes, even to rescue my lungs. Some people die from a smoking addiction. I was convinced that I would die from my passion for photography drawing me into that rat poison room.

Believe me when I say this, I was IN LOVE with photography as a young girl. At the lunch table, my girlfriends would talk about their boyfriends, crushes, and fantasies. I'm not trying to say I wasn't part of that crowd, but boys were not part of my priorities at the time- it was photography and only photography. It was the major thing that consumed my energy and time. It transformed me into a humanitarian artist. I wanted to expose issues that were ignored by mainstream media. I desired to create images and projects that were thought provoking, touching, inspirational, and improve the world we live in.

At fourteen, I was determined to transform how mass media effected females of all ages. During that time in my life, I was upset with society for not resisting the massive amounts of degrading female images that filled our lives. In teen magazines, I would see ads with young women's bodies completely exploited. Corporations were promoting sexual content more than their product. Shoe companies had young slender female models dressed in bikinis or undergarments taking up about ninety percent of their ads and wearing a pair of shoes. A small logo on the corner of the page was the only clue that it was a shoe advertisement. Television advertisements and shows weren't innocent either. The majority of the time they made our society look like everybody is sexually active and living in a soap opera world. Even listening to popular music on radio's top ten lists was not always so uplifting, because the lyrics would tell a girl to treat their body in a certain way to gain self-esteem and encourage guys to say and treat girls as sexual objects. Much of the movie industry, musical artists, and corporations do not take responsibility for the devastation it causes in our culture. Sex sells and young girls and women are victims of this product.

For many generations the media has relentlessly targeted the female population by falsely depicting them as degraded subjects and sexual objects. The media creates pressure upon young girls to meet expectations that match their ideal vision. For example, a skinny body, perfect skin and complexion, clothes showing as much skin as possible, and exposing part of your butt and/or breasts is desirable. This kind of misleading education is costly to us. The bombardment of media's deceptive projection on society forms distorted expectations towards females of all ages and eventually girls' and women's idea of themselves are psychologically alter. This poison is polluting our society. Poor values persist to be glorified: sex, violence, materialism, and appearance are glamorized in deceitful ways that distorts the self-image of developing young women and men. These dehumanizing images lead people into promiscuous and unwholesome lifestyles and cause psychological damage. But, obviously sex sells; mainstream media and corporations profit from destroying our values.

As participating consumers of their goods we allow them to victimize us with a false sense of appreciation towards self and culture. We need to make the right decisions to accept what is beneficial to our society, so we do not destroy what we have built. By rejecting media that degrades us and supporting media that elevates our self-esteem, a revolution in mass media can occur to change how females are portrayed. You, as the consumer and audience will have more input into their output.

All this has led me to educate myself more and more to comprehend the logic behind media's stereotypical branding of young girls and how it affects our culture. Many people seem to be unaware of the heavy psychological effect media has on our self-esteem and image. Reading, watching, and attending workshops on this subject fueled me with motivation to fight against this issue. As a fourteen-year-old photographer, I was determined to make a difference by capturing the truth and celebrating REAL young women. This is how Young Sisters was born to share genuine and positive images and stories of adolescent girls. This book is an important tool to speak up against misguided influence on females, and most importantly teenage girls.

To launch Young Sisters, I started to reach out my peers, put up flyers in different high schools, make announcements in classrooms, and advertise through word-of-mouth in cafeterias. During my travels, I searched for teenage girls who shared my vision and asked for participation. This book was a gateway for me to understand, sympathize, bond, and grow with girls in my age group. Every one had their own testimony to share about life's trials and successes.

Young Sisters is a brief introduction to the journeys female adolescents face. These moments are intended to boost young women's self-esteem, empower, bond, inspire, and invite them into others' lives through their peers' experiences. It allows teenage girls to celebrate being true to themselves. It's a tool enabling them to reach out to their peers and society. It presents an opportunity for society to deepen its understanding of the 21st century's young woman's diverse lifestyles.

Rise Up Sisters

Born and raised in the United States, I know I am very blessed, because of all the opportunities available to me. I had free public education, participated in after school programs, and received scholarships making it possible for me to attend college. This may seem standard for anyone pursuing an education in the United States; in other less developed countries such opportunities are only accessible to wealthy people. Although public education is not always the best, at least it's free, and it's something we should take advantage and make the most of. An educated person has options in society. The more you know, the more choices you have in making career choices and life decisions. Embrace education!

Throughout my childhood, my grandma reminded me of how fortunate I was to go to school, because she was not allowed to go to school in her homeland, China. Her father would tell her, "You are a girl, you should stay at home and work. I don't want to waste my money on your education because you will marry and become another person's property." As a young girl my grandma would collect sticks to sell as firewood, and on her way home, she would stop by the school and stand outside listening to the teacher and observing the class. Standing on the steps of that school was the closest she ever came to being in a classroom. Because my grandma was deprived of an education it made me appreciate the opportunities I was given even more.

She would constantly tell me, "Too bad I could not go to school when I was young. I would have a better job than working at a garment factory or being a janitor in the movie theater. People would not take advantage of me or make fun of me. If only I had an education, I would be able to read and write. Without an education, I missed out on a lot of things."

Growing up, these stories were constant reminders of how blessed I was, but it wasn't until a mission trip to Guyana, South America, that I realized how many people lack the opportunity to attend school. I witnessed real poverty for the first time in my life in this third-world country. I met a fifteen-year-old girl with her baby boy and her sixteen-year-old sister-in-law who was pregnant with her first child. They came from very poor families. As a result, they were fated to become mothers and housewives, because they did not have the money to pay for an education. After talking to those girls, I began to talk to local people about the educational norms in their country. The more people I spoke with, the more my heart began to ache, because everybody had the same answer: "Education is free until age fifteen or sixteen. We cannot afford to pay for our children's higher education. Most girls become housewives, because they cannot afford to go to school." Some of these adolescent girls accept the results of their poverty, but many of them were ambitious. They were eager to achieve a higher education with the hopes of fulfilling their dreams. Unfortunately, there is a wall called money that stops many of those girls from accomplishing their goals in life.

I recognize that resources are limited to young girls overseas and even some places here in the United States. For these reasons, I have decided to use a portion of the proceeds from Young Sisters to support scholarship funds for teenage girls living in poor areas of the world who would otherwise be deprived of an opportunity to attend higher education to fulfill their dreams. Another portion of the proceeds will be utilized to aid existing beneficial programs for teenage girls here in the US. Our government continuously cuts back on our education systems and programs for children. Money taken out from after school programs heightens the chance of teenagers joining the wrong crowds and prevents them from discovering their talents and developing self-worth. The money that has been taken out needs to be reinvested and dispersed wisely in our schools and after school programs so that our youth are not shortchanged from a quality education and from setting higher goals for their future. Budget cuts jeopardize the school environment learning facilities with an array of resources.

I feel it is everyone's responsibility to resolve the education crisis we are faced within America and abroad. I recommend donating our time, resources, money, and be involved with beneficial petitions. We can offer free tutoring, donate used books or school supplies overseas or to our local academic centers, give financial support to creditable youth organizations, and join campaigns that try to improve the education system.

Young Sisters helps provide funding for scholarships and support adolescent programs, which are meant to open doors for today and tomorrow's youth. Young people represent the future, and how we nurture them is how our world will become. Young Sisters celebrates our youth. Young Sisters' products contribute to a worthy cause and hope to make a difference in our youth and society. Collectively, you and I as a team will create a better present and future.

"What ever I do I always feel I want to help others."

Anonymous 19

Giving Back To Society

Anonymous 19

How old are you?
19

Are you in college?
Yes, first year, upper freshmen.

What is your major?
Undecided right now, it's between psychology and law.

What do you want more?
I guest I'm leaning more towards psychology, because its more people oriented than law. Even though you also deal with people as a lawyer. But in psychology, I think there is a line that you cross, where in law there are certain lines that you cross after a certain period of time doing cases and that is not what I want to do.

What made you interested in doing psychology?
I want to know why people behave the way they do. I figure it will give me a broader understanding of human beings as individuals. Why things happen? Why certain things happen? The cause of certain things. Frenetic science is also something that interests me. So from that, I want to study psychology.

When did you started to get interested in psychology?
My last year in high school, I was in a criminal justice academy. I wanted to know something else besides law and we did a lot of frenetic science. That has to do a lot with breaking down evidence and some of the frenetic science, look at criminal's behavior and that is also psychologist, frenetic psychologist. And I like that, so from that I was interested in learning why people behave the way they do. I also had to be sure that there is nothing else out there that I'm missing from before I actually decided, "Ok, law is for me." *Because I don't want to be anywhere where I am unhappy. You don't do your best when you are unhappy.*

Where do you want to be a psychologist?
It depends, because I like working with children. I definitely would enjoy working with children. I can do child psychology. I would think it would be interesting to work with criminals, with criminal psychology or to have my own office. I would like to have my own office, where clients could come in, but I don't have a specific field in psychology where I am heading towards. Right now, it's just a broad view of psychology, since its only my first year.

Are you enjoying it?
Yeah. Its interesting. I have good teachers. The teacher I had, he was pretty good and he made the class very interesting. There are certain things that I'm like, "Wow, I heard of that name before." But he went into it with more detail with the psychology class so I found that to be interesting. Like Sigmund Fraud, there is a theory of how a young boy is in love with his mother, and if there is a father there, he would be jealous of the father. He would feel all protective of the mother. I don't know if you have ever seen that with little boys. But I'm like, "Ok, I understand, cause I see little boys try to be over protective of their mothers." That's just like a general view of it.

Are you using psychology with your friends or family?
I try not to, because I was suggested not to. Since I'm not a specialist. We only got a broad view of it. There's nothing that we went into detail. So I try not to do that. There's things that I see that remind me of certain terms of psychology, but I try not to associate any of them with my friends or family.

Why do you want to be a psychologist?
Because I want to help people. What ever I do, I always feel I want to help others. Because I feel some people know the answers to their own problems, but they just haven't realize it yet. And I feel like, if I can help you realize the answer to your problems then you'll lead a better life or a happier life. At least I help you in some way and I want to help people.

"I believe girls/women have the power to do anything especially change the media image of women, or anything else as long as we are true to ourselves."

Renee 17

Media

Kadedra 18

We're going to discuss how I want to have plastic surgery.
Well, now a days you have to be *skinny* and be very attractive to even be notice. Especially in my profession as an actor or as anything in the entertainment business. If you wanna dance, if you wanna model, if you wanna act. You have to be slender and perfect and ordinary people are not. So I figure plastic surgery will be a easier way to achieve those goals. Because no matter how much you exercise, if you are not meant to be major thin then you are not meant to be. But if you have to do it by any means necessary.

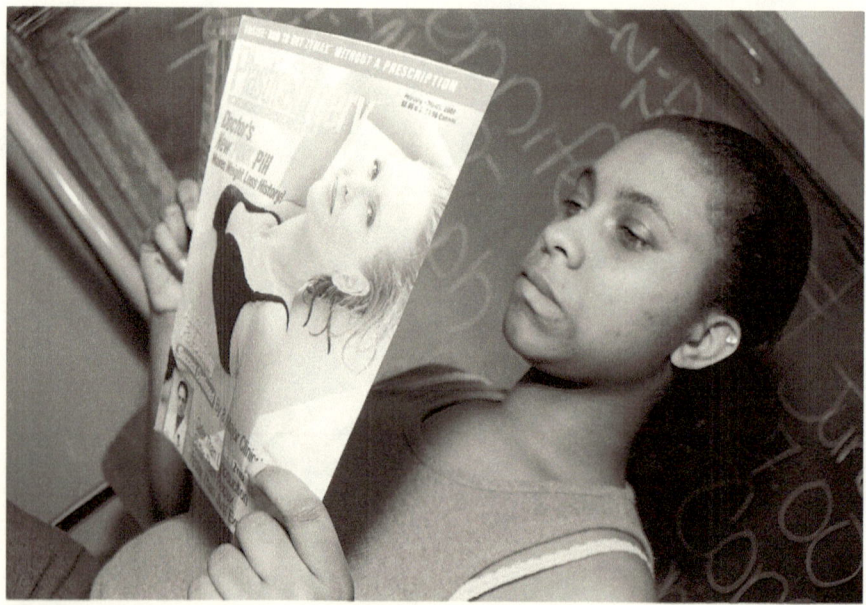

There are plenty of stars I would like to look, like Destiny Child. Look at Beyonce, she is like beautiful to the media. She has perfect skin, she's thin with long hair. Obviously that is what I am not, but you got to be beautiful if you want to succeed.

That's what you believe? You don't believe it's the talent that you have?
I believe somewhat is talent, but the thing is, if you don't have the right look it doesn't matter how much talent you have.

Do you believe there's a lot of people in the media field who are not talented but they have the looks and that is why they are so famous.
O yes, there are plenty of people like that. I feel that the acting business is so hard, because first of all, people like me and you or anybody else who wants to pursue acting, who has great talent. If you're fat, or if your too skinny or you are too tall, certain characters, certain scenes, and certain people don't want to put you in their movie, because you don't have "the look."

How do you feel about yourself? Are you satisfied with how you look? Like not just…

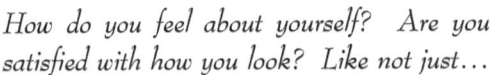

talking about doing what you wanna do to look a certain way.
Outside of that, I'm…I mean I'm okay with myself. There are certain things I know I could work on for myself. So its like, I'm okay. My self-esteem is not that high, but its not that low either.

Do you feel like you are a media disappointment?
Yes, I do. There have been plenty auditions that I've went to and even the casting director said, "I did great, but I don't have the look." And the next thing you find out who they showed, it was somebody with big breast, long legs, long hair, light skin and no pimples and no stretch marks and no ounce of fat anywhere with the acting level of a pea. Its not worth it.
I mean, I can say that big models and big actors are coming up, but they are still not being recognize for their acting skills. Its like we have a couple of actors such as the girl who plays Kim on channel 11, she could sing and she's big and she can act. They won't put her on movies because of that.

But seeing her on TV does it give you some kind of hope that you might make it into the media business because of how you look?
Yeah, a little hope. But you know what will give me more hope is that if they allow her to do more stuff. I mean she talked about it on TV how she audition for movies and everything. They just are telling her that she doesn't have the right look. So I guess there is always a point where you can make it just a little bit just to get your foot in the door.

Young Sisters

Are you willing to pay the price of thinness like bulimic, anorexia, exercising all day and starving yourself?
No.

Have you ever tried it before?
Nahhh. I've tried exercising all day, just because I was out of shape. If I walk up two steps then I'm tired that's why I tried exercising to get back into shape. But, nahhh.

Does people's opinion on how you look effect you?
Yes. On certain days being a women, you like to hear, "Hey, you're pretty" or "That's nice." I don't care if people are like, "O, that's pretty, that's not pretty." Its just nice to hear once in the blue moon.

When you look at a shopping magazine, instead of shopping for clothes you want to shop for their bodies? Even though she has on a nice pair of pants, but you want her legs.
Yeah, I do that most of the time. Like I love Tyra Banks, but I feel there's some imperfections about her body I wouldn't like. I'll shop shop on people. Like I want Jennifer Anderson's hair, I want Tyra Bank's legs or Jada Pinkett's stomach. Yeah I do that often, but I don't let it really get to me, because some of those things are unrealistic for me.

Because of your self-image do you feel insecure?
Yes, because...around where I live I get the most ridicule and when I go to auditions it gets even worse. Its like when people know you...cause I always didn't look like this. It wasn't until I hit puberty where everything started filling in. So they are used to seeing the tall slinky Kadedra and that is what they thought was beautiful. So when I used to do things like that when I was little, I used to get all the auditions. I used to get, "O, you're so pretty." And now that I go back to the same people that audition me before telling me how beautiful I am, now they are like, "You need to trim down, you need to lose thirty pounds."

Are you willing to do that to get the part?
Nah. Not really.

So were you serious about getting plastic surgery?
In a way I was until recently. I figured I got to start first. If I want to love me or if I want other people to love me, I have to love me first.

When you hear people in the media who got any type of surgery like nose and boob surgery, how do you feel about them like what's you image of them?
I feel like Pamela Anderson Lee, she had her breasts done a long time ago and she became really famous. But ever since they busted and she took them out and her breasts look big already. I feel like why do that, that's very... stupid. Why would you mess up your body if it was perfect already.

Do you feel if you would have done surgery, then your body will be perfect- like media perfect?
Yeah, I do.

Do you feel like in America, they make girls feel insecure, like being insecure is in and confident is out about how we feel about our body?
No, I feel that the media is portraying... I feel like the skinny girls they put out there is what they want everybody else to look like, but yet they are saying that confidence is cool and to love yourself. But if they really want us to love ourselves then why not put people out there that look like us. Out of ten people you see walking down the street, you only see one, really thin and nice looking compared to the media nice looking. The rest of us are average and yet I don't see any average models out there and any average actors out there making it.

Do you feel being different is a gift and you enjoy your self-image now?
Now I do, but if you were to ask me this question about four months ago, I would've tell you, "I feel disgusting, I hate myself. I'm fat."

So what made you like yourself?
I figure is all about understanding yourself. I figured that if you want anybody to take you seriously you can't go to auditions thinking that you're fat or you're ain't going to get the part, because of this and that. You got to have confidence in yourself and say I can do this and I'm fine. And you have to love yourself before anybody else can love you. I have cool friends and people who accept me for who I am and not for what I look like.

So that boosted up your confidence a lot?
A lot.

Do you know that on magazines when you see a picture it is not the actual model? They actually digitized their hair and bigger boobs and skinner body. Did you know that?
I'm just finding that out.

If you didn't know about this would you feel like every girl in this planet looks like that?
I wouldn't feel like every girl in this planet looks like that because, "Hey, look at me." I would feel that ... it did waken me a lot that to know that even they don't look that good. They're striving to be better looking than they are and I think they're perfect.

Lets talk about media and self image. Like on the magazine, you didn't even know that its not the real model they actually did all this digitizing. How has it had a negative impact on you?
O man, it has a *way* negative impact on me, because I look at myself and first of all *the guys* our age look at the books too and they are like I want a girl like this, she's perfect in every way. And that makes it hard for me to date, because guys our age are looking for model girls and we're not model girls. And people tend to look at you if you are more prettier than other girls you tend to be more successful. So I figure if I don't look like this girl on this magazine I'm not going to ever get anywhere in life.

Do you have anything to add?
All this stuff I've been through, I've been dealing with this stuff for a long time. Hating myself, loving myself. I finally figure that in order to get any where in life, in order to be truly successful and have a happy life, you have to love yourself and if you don't love yourself then that is a problem. You have to learn and do many things to strive to get to know yourself better, because thats the only true way you could be happy or truly think you're beautiful.

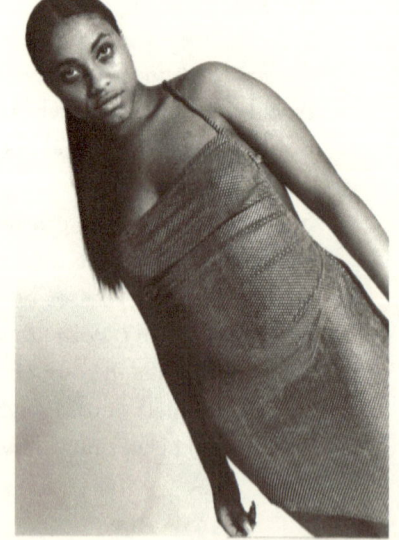

Kadedra

I remember everything about my anorexia.
Skipping meals, running around the neighborhood
with five layers on, endless crunches and pushups.
But what I remember most of all was
the endless self-loathing I felt every time I looked
in the mirror or saw my reflection in a
store window. The feeling of failure - to my
friends, family, and most of all to our society. A
society where girls like Christina Aguilera are
worshipped for their impossibly perfect bodies. While
Girls like me struggle every day to be recognized in
our society as hot, sexy, beautiful. These feelings
were what ignited my anorexia. My first thoughts
of feeling fat began one day when I was hanging
out with my boyfriend. I'm sure he didn't mean
anything by it, but he poked my stomach and
told me I had a gut. Even tho he wasn't serious
I went home that night, and took off my shirt
and stared at the mirror. As I looked, I saw
myself with a gut. I saw myself as fat. I
couldn't deal with that. I had always been the
perfect skinny one. I had to lose weight. I began
making plans. First. Start running every day. Second.
It's a pain in the ass to pack a lunch, so just
skip it. Third. Suck in my gut every whenever
possible. I figured I'd be thin again in a couple days.
No such luck. I struggled with my first plan for
a weeks. Then my boyfriend dumped me. I thought
for sure he didn't like me anymore because I was
fat. Why else would we have broken up? It was
clear to me that I needed a new plan. Since skipping
lunch wasn't doing anything, how about skipping
breakfast too? No one would notice anyway. So

Young Sisters

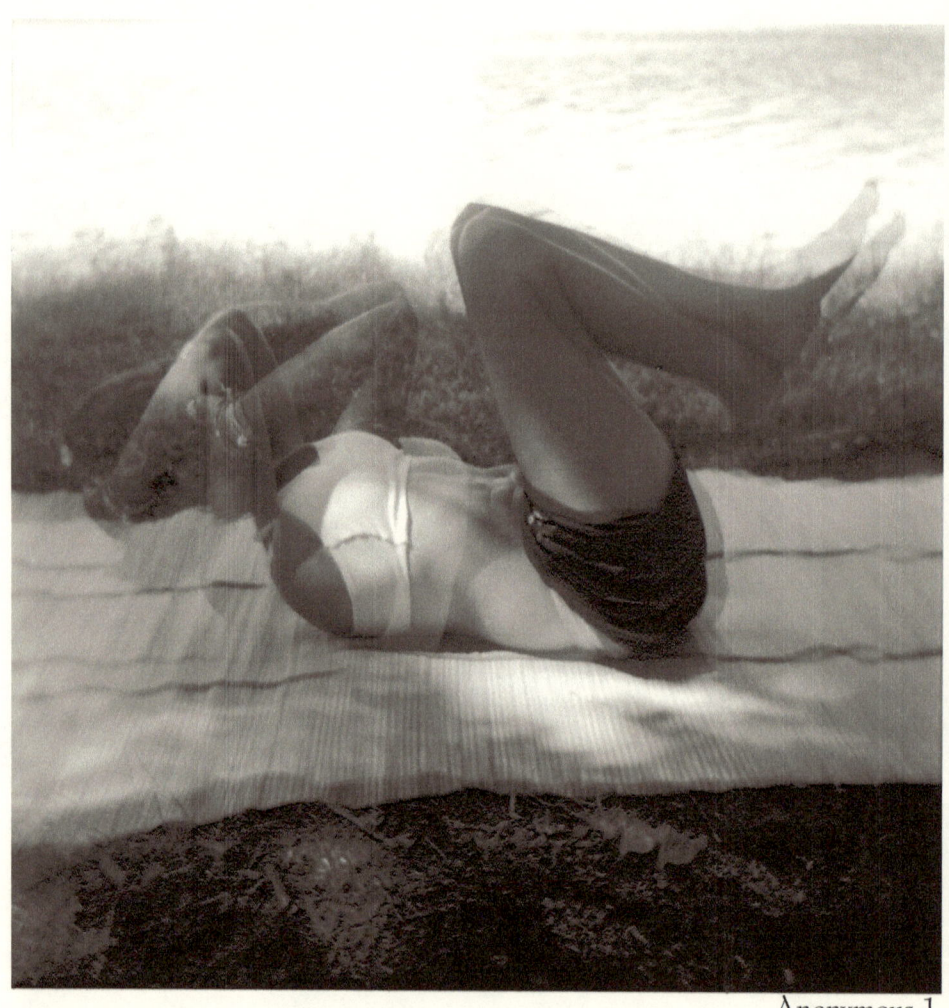

Anonymous 1

from then on, I only ate dinner. At first it killed me not to eat. I was constantly craving food and would never let myself have it. After a while my metabolism slowed down. Even eating a granola bar made me feel fat. I had no energy. When I came home from school I went straight to bed. My grades slipped and it became harder and harder to pay attention in class. I dreaded going to school, where I would be forced to look at everyone else's perfect bodies and where I couldn't show off my own. I became more depressed as the days passed. January changed to February, February to March and my eating disorder progressed. One night after an exhausting day of running, crunches, and situps, ~~Thursay~~ my mom and I had a huge fight. My mom and I have never really gotten along, but my depression made it 10 times worse. ~~And that~~ I couldn't tell you what it was about. All I remember about this fight was that afterwards, I rummaged through my father's drawers to find his knife. It was the first ~~time~~ I'd ever cut myself. It was painful, I want lie. But the relief ~~as~~ I felt, ~~no~~ was worth it, ~~$~~ or so I thought at the time. I didn't realize it at the time but eating disorder was affecting me more psychologically than physically. All I knew at the time was that slowly but surely I was losing weight, even if I didn't see the difference. March was a rough month, friends, guys, and parents were acting stupid. Over spring break ~~off~~ I had an "epiphany". One morning my parents and grandma drove out to a little beach town. The hotel we stayed at offered a buffet. Instead of my usual eggs and bacon that I order at hotels, I picked up a

Young Sisters

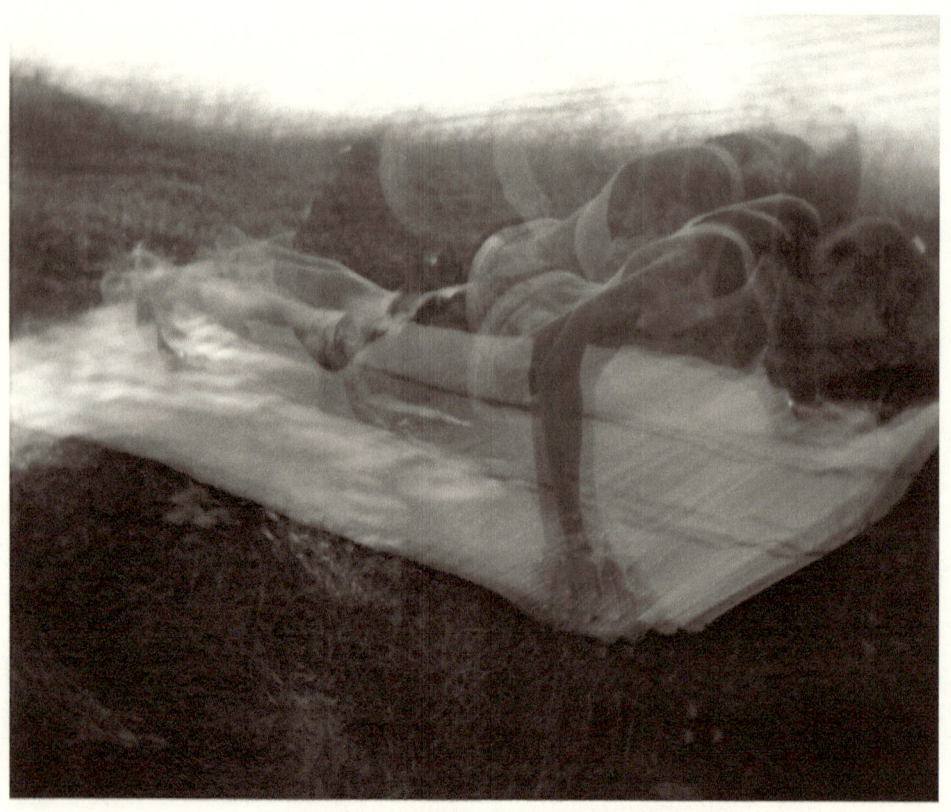

box of Special K. The box said "lose 6 pds. in 2 weeks". My heart jumped at the sight of those words. I ate a box and some fruit with it, to feel healthy. After that meal, I felt something I hadnt felt in a long time. Or maybe it was the absence of something. The absence of feeling fat. I felt strong and healthy. I dont know how that one little meal could have made me so happy, but it did. That wasnt the end of my eating disorder, but it was a start. I wont go into all the details of my recovery, but I started seeing a very nice therapist and I joined the softball team. That summer I dyed my hair pink and I felt on top of the world. I met two wonderful boys at camp, one from Massachusetts, the other from California. I went on a long awaited and hard worked on trip to Wyoming with my girl scout trip, two years in the planning. I enjoyed a summer at the pool with my friends. It was the best summer of my life, hands down. So I discovered that life does go on after a setback. I still have fat days however and I know that my anorexia will still follow me, but I accept it as part of who I am and I dont let it get me down. I dont strive to be just like anyone else, even my idol Gwen Stefani. I've learned that just because everyone in Hollywood is "perfect" doesnt mean I have to be too. I am "perfect" in my own eyes.

Renée
Age = 17

" As a teenaged girl I feel bothered by advertising images of skinny, tall models with clear faces and manicured nails and perfect guys with chiseled, cut muscles. I don't like the false kind of advertising that's directed towards me, telling me not to do drugs, sex, and cigarettes; but in movies like "House Party" and "Can't Hardly Wait" telling me to be a rowdy, rebellious teen. It's all hypocritical and it seems so fake. There are so many different kinds of people in the world that the media shouldn't project one image. I am a petite, passionate, opinionated, bi-cultural dancer. If I'm looking through the pages of a magazine, some of the girls seem to be independent and fierce, trying to stand out from the crowd. Usually, though, most girls in a magazine just look pretty; the pictures don't celebrate the great things about being a young woman that have nothing to do with looks. You can be a skateboarder, a golfer, a partner in a law firm, and be an entrepreneur. You don't have to rely on men. As tacky as that may sound, it's true. I believe girls/women have the power to do anything esspecially change the media image of women, or anything else as long as we are true to ourselfs.

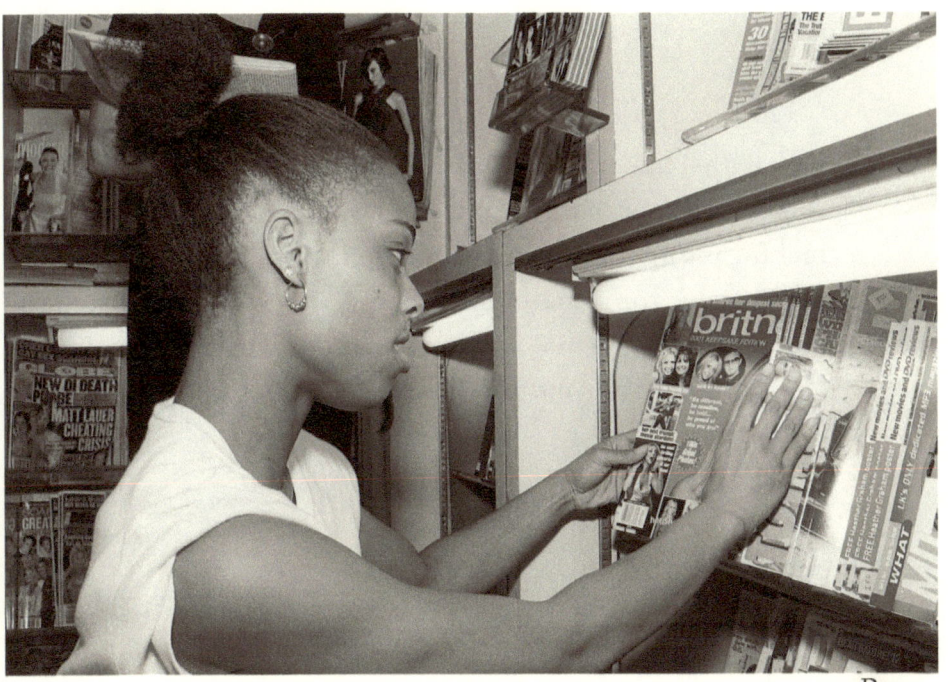

Renee

"What the camera has captured I will never be able to achieve without makeup and good lighting. Rather than making me appreciate myself, this photograph has forced me to strive for something elusive. However, it has also made me realize that I have to accept what I cannot change and given me the courage to alter what I can - my mind."

Flonia 18

Self Image

Flonia 18

If you were to go back in time which decade would you pick?
I pick the 1820s, no kidding. (Smiles) I'll pick the 1940s.

Why?
Why? Well...I really love the movies. I basically grew up on black and white films. Marilyn Monroe, Marlene Dietrich, Gary Cooper, Cary Grant. I can go on and on. I pick the 1940s, because I think I'm an old soul. Seriously. You know, I don't if people believe in reincarnation and all that bullshit. People have different personalities. You can feel your personality right? Like the way you walk. Well, I don't know, I feel like mine is old fashion, not old fashion like I'm a home girl bullshit kind of stuff like that. I mean old fashion in the sense that I like the old era. The golden era of Hollywood. I like that sort of era. Not to live in necessary in the day-to-day life. That's the kind of era I would like to be in if I were ever to go back to live. But I wouldn't be a housewife though; I will be the bombshell you know. I would be an actress, I would be Marilyn Monroe. I would want to act. I want that type of lifestyle. That glamorous life that they depict on silver screen.

Do you plan to be an actress?
That used to be one of my goals. That used to be my only goal like two years ago. But, now I switch gears. I still want to act. But I'm looking towards directing more. I can act in my own films, make myself into a 1940s bombshell.

Who inspired you watching old movies, was it your parents?
Um, I grew up in Albania, for the first half of my childhood, for nine years. That was the type of programs they had on the channels. They had black and white...not only Hollywood movies, but that was what I was introduced to.

Since you talk so much about the old Hollywood style would you go back and copy some of their styles they have for Hollywood movies?
My plan is not to make Hollywood movies actually, I want to make my own films. I want to be independent. But definitely, if I were ever to make a movie base in that time period, of course. It wasn't only Hollywood style, that was the decade. Yes, Hollywood turn out a lot of the images, but that was the decade, that was the image.

What do you love most about the 1940s?
I think there is a certain feeling that is associated with every decade. I think that the decade that we are talking about had so much sensuality and sex and....mystery and mysticism, and all that aura of like the noire films they all represented that era. The feel of the decade is what attracts me to it. For example in the 1950s, they were about dancing and the big poodle skirts and all that stuff, but that's not me. I like the more sensuous, slow walk, deep voice, smoke, style...

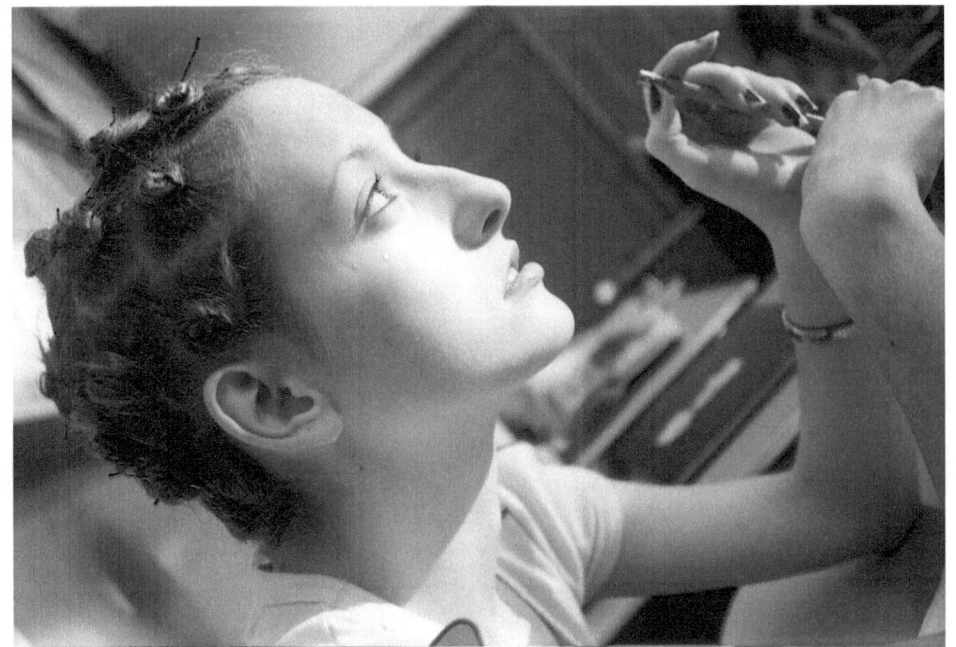

Flonia

Young Sisters

I remember posing for this picture. I remember the two dozen red and pink roses Anna and I bought for the shoot. Too bad the picture is in black and white and you can't see their beautiful color. I remember that we had the radio on and we were giggling and chatting loud enough to disrupt the photography class going on in the next studio. I remember the linen sheet that was ruined because we got baby oil all over it. To this day my mom does not know it's missing. I remember thinking about how good I looked when Anna first showed this picture to me. Black and white film performs wonders. What I think the camera is able to accomplish at given times is capturing how our ideal self would look like as opposed to our flawed self. My skin looks flawless. There is no trace of my large pores nor is there trace of the black and blue bags under my sunken eyes. Everything from the rose petals, to my hand, my face and my hair has been carefully lit and positioned so that the look of beauty can be achieved.

Two years later I find myself disliking what this photo represents. It is not me in this picture. Rather, the subject is an artificial and idealized version of myself. I don't appreciate what the picture portrays or represents. What the camera has captured I will never be able to achieve without makeup and good lighting. Rather than making me appreciate myself, this photography has forced me to strive for something elusive. However, it has also made me realize that I have to accept what I cannot change and given me the courage to alter what I can — my mind.

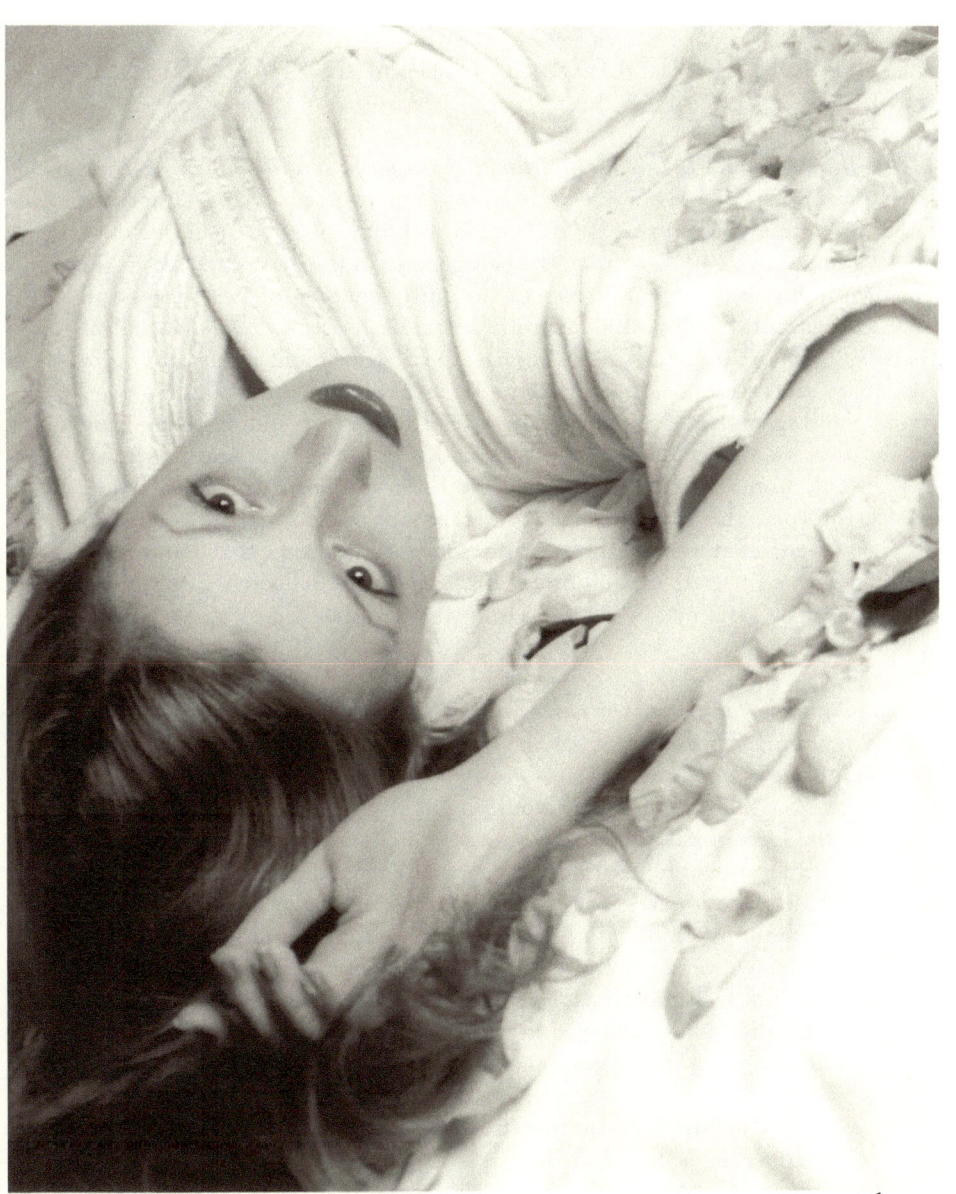

Flonia

Naomi
LIFE THROUGH THE LENS OF BOHEMIAN RHAPSODY AND ECCELESIASTES

Is this the real life? Is this just fantasy? Caught in a landslide, no escape from reality... Hi! My name is Sophia. I'm trapped in the American Dream. "Trapped!" you say, "Why, Sophia, you have it all!" Yeah, maybe I do. We've got two cars — one in the garage, one in the driveway. We've got our own home, mortgaged, of course, a family made up of two successful, powerful parents, a dog, and a pretty affluent lifestyle. We live better than 99.99% of the world. My family and I, you might argue, are quite free from starvation, fear, or any type of lack whatsoever. Why, we even have spending money, so that we can afford to be free and easy any time we choose. Recreation comes in all forms for us — movies, music, shows, dinner out, home entertainment, sports: both spectator and participant, books, internet, the fine arts, vacations abroad, everything! We have no physical needs that remain unmet, no social aspirations that cannot be fulfilled with a little effort, and no craving, whether intellectual or physical, that cannot be satiated. What's so confining about being totally satisfied, you want to know?

Open your eyes, look up to the skies and see... No one has ever pinned down a concrete, uniform definition of the American Dream. I remember that the evening news once ran a series on the American Dream, on how it was receding faster than the general populace could grab it. According to this channel, the Dream was something along the lines of having a house, a car, a good family, a decent household income, and a reasonably adequate ability to keep up with the Joneses. Or was it? I remember there never being any mention of the Joneses, but since then, every newspaper and newsmagazine article that I have read on the issue has mentioned keeping up with the Joneses. My family, I know, has never really followed trends. For the most part, we're satisfied where we are, and we have no burning desire nor drive to engage in one-upping the neighbors, or society at large.

What exactly did they say during those reports? I remember the clip of a man throwing a football to his son on their lush, green lawn, in front of a well-kept, large, white house with a garage that had a car. (As of 2001, that car would be a sport utility vehicle.) It has only been a few years since they aired it, but things have changed so much. All right, I must say upon reconsideration, ten years have passed from then to now. What I was just saying was that things have certainly changed — we've witnessed the SUV craze, the rise and fall of internet and tech-related stocks, the emergence of a pop culture where ever younger superstars burst onto the teen scene, and the rise of a class of adolescents that are enjoying resources and wealth on an unprecedented level in American history. Yet, how much of this is true? This is what the media tells us is going on with most of the country, but in reality, most of the country can't afford to live like I or the rest of the American upper middle class do. There are still many people who live below the poverty line, whether they are deep in inner cities or deep in rural backwoods. All of the popular trends that I mentioned — SUV's, stocks, teenybopper culture, rich adolescents, can be patronized only by those that have a fairly substantial amount of discretionary income. The rest of the country just doesn't have the money to play along.

I'm just a poor boy, I need no sympathy, because I'm easy come, easy go, little high, little low... I read in a magazine for older adults that the Dream was financial security, and the ability to maintain independence for as long as possible. I see how that works — I mean, after all, everyone has wants, and everyone has needs, and naturally, their desires reflect their lack. A large segment of the older population, though, really is destitute, or at least not secure enough to be comfortable. They don't have enough money to rise above substandard living in some cases, but often don't have the ability to amend the situation. The American work ethic that says that nothing beats hard work for making a good life doesn't seem to apply in the situation that the elderly face. They are willing to work, as evidenced by the fact that they are more dependable than their younger counterparts, but age discrimination is a problem that is not easy to overcome. Employers, who are supposed to be evaluating their employees and potential workers based solely on talent, expertise, and suitability for the job, are yet considering the extra factor of age, and it's just not fair! Ah, but in today's dog-eat-dog world, does fairness really have value? Some would say that it's just an abstract value, but it's almost un-American to say that, somehow. Fairness is linked with honesty, and no one the world over likes a dishonest person, deep down. Ultimately, though, does honesty help the bottom line? It might, if the consumers are educated enough about business practices to care that they are good and humane. But then again, we see lots of dishonest businesses getting ahead through use of prison labor in foreign countries, sweatshop labor in outsourced locales, stuff like that.

My dad said that the Dream is about having stuff. What I inferred when I put that statement in the context of all the other stuff he says about money and the way Americans handle it was something along the lines of: Americans want to get rich quick, but our family tradition has been to get knowledge. I once responded, "But having people in your family, and educating them, is expensive! It costs a lot to raise kids."

He replied, "Yes, but people make money. How are you going to get rich if you don't have human capital?" I was slightly confused. So he valued higher education over the quick money that could be made from jobs taken right after high school. Right. And in general he saw Americans as people who wanted to get rich quick, often for little work. Something for nothing, he said. This was the same person, though, who told me to pursue law or medicine so that I would have a comfortable, no, superb lifestyle, one that would certainly be full of money. Somehow, he could mention all of these conflicting things in the same eight-minute conversation, as he often did.

To me, he was making a good salary. Our living expenses were low, and he got to sock away a lot of his monthly paycheck. However, he would often complain about "how difficult it [was] just to survive." I would ask my mother, "What's he talking about?" and ask him, "What are you talking about? This is a pretty comfortable lifestyle. Don't you like the way that we're living now? It's pretty good!" I wonder if he really meant his complaints, or if he just talked without thinking too much. If the case was the former, then life is pretty sad — a person can have all of his needs met, and yet not appreciate the bounty around her. Even in abundance, humans will complain. What's the point of riches and material wealth if humans will continue to complain even with an abundance of them?

I take it that the American Dream was not his dream, not in its entirety, not without emendation. Sometimes I try to work out some sort of system where his principles would all work together and form rules that he lives by, just to see if I can understand him better and know where he's coming from. After all, he is my dad. It's a bit forced, but here's my theory of what's going on in his head:
Education now will have a big payoff later
Education means forgoing quick cash now
Americans would rather have the quick cash now than the big payoff later
I would rather have the big payoff later, but it's later, now, and I haven't gotten the big payoff yet. It's coming, though. Something big is almost here. I'm on the verge of a big break.
Worse to worst, though, I can always get my daughter to make the big living that I never could because I was pursuing research that would help humankind. She'll take a path where it's easy to make a fortune, and we can all enjoy our lives.

Wisdom, like an inheritance, is a good thing and benefits those who see the sun. Wisdom is a shelter as money is a shelter, but the advantage of knowledge is this: that wisdom preserves the life of its possessor.

So, basically, we had all the components of the news media's Dream, but they didn't constitute my father's Dream. His dream and the media's dream were different. Ah, the media, the media, the media. The media are the ones that portray the ideal as youth, wealth, and beauty. The media's images are inescapable. The media. They make it seem that the Dream should be all about having a beautiful body, a beautiful face, and beautiful friends. Beautiful cars, houses, and possessions, would not hurt, either. I often worry that Hollywood has invaded the minds of Americans who don't think for themselves. MTV has become the surrogate advisor of choice for the naive youths who have little experience discerning who has their best interests in mind. MTV listens because it has a vested interest in the young people of today. If their spending power and their desirability as a market were not such a draw, MTV would not be so powerful. It's complicated, I know, but ultimately this type of relationship is a circular one: young people support MTV because it supports them. MTV listens to young people because they sustain it. Marketers listen to MTV because they are greedy for the dollars of young people. Young people like this attention from the marketers and from MTV, regardless of their avaricious motivations. Money buys attention and fawning, but that's partially because young people's attentions are very much in demand and considered to be worth a premium. Where is the love in this cycle? Who is looking out for the best interests of the young generation? The parents?

I sometimes wish I'd never been born at all... One day, while I was online, an IM window popped up on my screen. The conversation went something like this:

LilHamster: Hello
Everyman11: Who is this?
LilHamster: I'm no one you know.
LilHamster: I just picked you randomly
Everyman11: Oh
LilHamster: So
LilHamster: Let's talk
LilHamster: a/s/l?

I hesitated. Who was this person, anyway? But a/s/l was standard, so I figured that I had nothing to fear.

Everyman11: 16/f/NY
Everyman11: you?
LilHamster: 15/m/VA
LilHamster: hobbies?

Again, I stopped. Was this safe? I banked on the advice I'd gotten from a friend online — he'd met lots of people online, and he'd never had a bad experience.

Everyman11: reading, writing. You?
LilHamster: I think a lot
LilHamster: Sometimes I just can't fall asleep, I'm lying there in bed, thinking
LilHamster: I mean, I don't know
LilHamster: Lately I've been really tired
LilHamster: Because I've been thinking so much
LilHamster: But I don't really know, I mean,
LilHamster: life is just so..

Wow. This was a lot for a first encounter. Most of my friends never talked about such things when we chatted online. Perhaps they were not up to sharing deep thoughts with me. Most of them, I take it, were too occupied with schoolwork and sleep deprivation to think much. But then again, I don't generally share my inmost thoughts with my friends, so should I expect that they share their deep and heavy thoughts with me?

LilHamster and I chatted about more mundane things like course selection, anime, and writing samples, in subsequent IMs which took place much later on. However, in the first week after that initial IM, every time I signed on, he would start a conversation, and sometimes I wondered if he was suicidal, the way he talked about thinking so much and losing sleep for contemplations.
LilHamster: So what's your favorite quote?
Everyman11: I have a lot of favorites, but this one means a lot to me
Everyman11: I've got to get it right, but it's something like, "The fields are ripe for harvest! Ask the Lord of the harvest to send out workers so nothing will be lost."
Everyman11: I forget the reference, exactly
Everyman11: Luke 10:2? Not quite
LilHamster: Oh, the Bible.
Everyman11: Yup.
LilHamster: Are you a Christian?
Everyman11: I am.
LilHamster: I'm an Orthodox Christian.
LilHamster: It's nice to think on these things, sometimes.

Mama, ooh, didn't mean to make you cry, if I'm not here again this time tomorrow... I met another guy, a Pastor Dave, and he was precocious. He made it to the tenth grade, tried junior year, found that it was too hard, and dropped out. At seventeen, he was walking around with wads of money in his back pocket, thousands of dollars, driving a two-year-old Cadillac, smoking the best dope, always being surrounded by girls. He had all the dope he wanted, he told us — he had it 'til it came out of his ears. Yet, there was still something — his heart — something there, nagging at him, refusing to go away — that hole in his heart —

He told us that it wasn't worth it. All that stuff, yeah, it gave him that rush, gave him that high, but what? One thing would come, he'd take it, and then the next, and the next... It was a never-ending cycle of torture. He liked the stuff, but deep down inside, he couldn't take it.

I met Pastor Dave and heard his story, and thought of LilHamster. Searching for something that he doesn't even know he needs, eh?

The fate of the fool will overtake me also. What then do I gain by being wise? Like the fool, the wise man must die! -- Ecclesiastes "I want to see you go to Yale and Harvard," said one of my cousins, patting my leg. "Yeah," said a second cousin who was sitting on my other side. "I can see that you're of that caliber." She patted my leg, too. It was like something out of Jane Austen: four girls who were three sisters, and their cousin, sitting in one room, plotting the future and success of the fourth. The ages were almost commensurate with those of the Bennet sisters, too — at twenty-seven and twenty-five, the oldest two, whom I'll call Jane and Elizabeth, were considered very marriageable. Then there was the third girl, whom I'll call Kitty (short for Catherine), who had just graduated from an Ivy League school. She was also eligible, at twenty-one, but was in no hurry to get married, especially when her sisters had not yet set a precedent. And then there's me. I'm like Lydia in age, but in most other aspects I'm like Mary. So what do I call myself? Sophia.

It was funny how, until recently, my best friend thought that my name meant "deceived," or "clever lie." After all, its root appears to be close to the root of "sophistry." In actuality, my name means "wisdom." How ironic, indeed. It's like wisdom and foolishness don't even matter; people think what they will, sometimes out of willful ignorance, and sometimes not.

The Bennet girls had some idea of what happiness would be for them. Jane knew that Bingley was for her, Elizabeth discovered that Darcy pleased her, and Lydia, Kitty, and Mrs. Bennet, found satisfaction in the young men of the militia, not least of all Mr. Wickham. Mrs. Bennet had an appreciable, incredibly delectable goal just in her sights, ready to be seized upon: the arrangement of profitable, noble marriages for her daughters, the eldest especially. I, on the other hand, do not have a clear goal at this point. Is Yale really my love and my all-abandoned pursuit? It seems not, but my family seems to be making it so in their opinions. My cousins and my father have started the matchmaking process and are appalled that, like Lizzie, I have initial doubt and repulsion.

God has made everything beautiful in its time. He has also set eternity in the hearts of men; yet they cannot fathom what God has done from beginning to end. -- Ecclesiates What if I should come to the end of my life and find that I've wasted all my time? No, that's too sudden. Let's try again. What if I should come to the end of my life? Okay, that's inevitable. I just don't feel it right now, being that I'm in my youth. I know in my mind that death can happen any time, any place, for any reason, but my heart doesn't believe it. My heart says that there's a tomorrow, and that tomorrow has its own tomorrow. That's why I'm planning so far in advance... college... it's not far off. Grad school... now that's far off. Somehow even getting a job in the real working world is more palatable to my sense of time than graduate school. It's like I'm myopic in that I can wonder about what I'll do, but I'm hyperoptic in that I don't know exactly what lies ahead, so I'm looking ahead to the certainties of work and family.

Not that work and family are such certainties, either? Things in my life change every week, even if nothing major has happened in my world. Simply receiving the newest batch of college viewbooks is enough to gently, but surely, blow with some force at the heretofore established solidity of my top twelve list. Suddenly, doubts arise: If I stick solely to these few schools and research them while disregarding all other college solicitations, will I miss out on anything? What if I could have made a better choice? That's a big one. The thing is, I may never know whether I could have chosen a more expedient path, for, as Robert Frost wrote, "Way leads on to way." On the other hand, knowing that today's college graduates move through several careers in a lifetime doesn't give me very much comfort. Logically, it should, because it would mean that no mistake I would make would be final, but this social upheaval just creates more uncertainty for me. But then again, ten years from now, according to a thirty-two year old genius friend, none of this will matter. Sure, sure. He went to MIT.

"Find the Absolute Rhythm and Follow it with Absolute Trust," said the Ohio University Honors Tutorial College's mail. I was moderately interested. Another Christian college, I thought, but one with more force and conviction, eh? When I had finished flipping through the pamphlet, I was both confused and amazed — confused because a secular school was making an absolute claim, and amazed that this school had the audacity to do so. I felt almost as if I'd flipped through some cult's literature... that certainty was weird, and I definitely didn't trust it.

All I want to know is that when my time is up, that I haven't wasted my life.

Nothing really matters, anyone can see; nothing really matters to me... Any way the wind blows... Meaningless, meaningless, everything is meaningless... a chasing of the wind... full of sound and fury, signifying nothing. But you know what? Pursuing Jesus changes everything.

"I didn't blame God for putting all those pains on me. But rather, I thanked Him in the end. If I never gone through something like that, I wouldn't have understood the pain, the misery, and the struggle. Now that I understand, I can use it to help others who are going through similar problems. ...He loves me, just as He loves everyone else in this world."

Fan 15

Religion

Fan   (age 15)

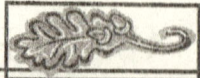

TESTIMONIAL

If anyone asks "Fan, who's your idol?" I would proudly reply, " GOD! WHO ELSE?!" But I would have had a different answer a year ago. Like everyone else, I wasn't born as a believer of God. Although some of my family members are followers of Buddhism, I would tell myself, "I don't need to believe in anything. Why should I?!" But all that was changed when I had my first encounter with God and stopped the aimless wonder I had for 13 years.

Around a year ago, I went to Camp Warwick with three of my friends from school along with the staff of CCHC. I went with my friends to have fun not learn about God. However, it rained the whole time. "Aw shucks!" I thought to myself. We didn't want to be locked indoor all the time since it's camp, I just wanted the rain to stop right there right then. But it didn't. Although it gotten smaller and smaller as the day passed by, the rain did not stop till the day we were leaving. At camp, we went to messages and heard about the stories of God and how God had helped even people from the present time. I didn't pay much attention to it all at first, but slowly, when the reverend began talking about the sense of emptiness and loneliness we all felt at time that nothing seems to be able to fill. I thought, " Wow... it's like he's talking to me!" Even though I grew up with a great family who loves me who offered me everything I should and could have. But even with the love and luxuries I owned, I still felt empty and lonely deep down in a part of me. When the reverend said God was the only one who is able to fill up the emptiness and sweep the loneliness away for us, I saw hope. But even with that hope, I still hesitated about believing in something I can't even see, hear, or feel. I shook my head and emptied my thought.

As the rain continued, I had a lot more time in my hands to gather up my thoughts since we couldn't go outdoors. As I lied in the bed one day, I quietly listened to the rain outside and a thought hit me. There was a reason for me to be here. There's also a reason for the rain; I came here to know about God, his love for me, and to finally find my way back to him. He had created me, he always loves me and with that love, he sacrificed his very own son Jesus Christ for we sinners who had done nothing but deceive him, disobey him and disappoint him. Although not many of us appreciated what he had done and continued to sin, he still didn't give up on us. He is still waiting for us to turn our heads and go back to him, even if only one out of trillions was still lost at the end, he would still ache for that one person. Because God is Love. When I realized all those things, I suddenly felt shameful for deceiving God all those times of my life. That same night, during another service, I accepted the Lord into my heart. The rest of the time at camp was terrific, I felt something more in me, something I can't quite describe. But it was this positive energy that not even the crummy weather could destroy. During my first year of high school, I developed symptoms of serious depression from pressures received from school, new environment, meeting new friends, and a lot of other issues and temptations faced by all teenagers. Not only that, I had another problem with my physical problem as well. Tremendous amount of pain occurred frequently which prevented me from going to school for 4 months. During those times, I was miserable. Sadness overcame me, tears filled my cheek and wet my pillows every night and every day. Countless times I thought about killing myself. One day, as I wept, I slowly walked into the kitchen, took out a knife and attempted to cut my wrist. When it touched my skin, I suddenly thought of God and my family. God had put me on earth for a purpose, before I fulfill my purpote, I cannot

die. Besides, my family, my parents, they loved me so much, they [my friends] would be devastated to find me dead. I can't do that to God, I can't do that to my family. But the head felt as if it was torn apart. Mental and physical pain urged me to end my life . I struggled and finally, I put down the knife. But that wasn't the only time that had happened. Everyday I had to put up with the pain and the struggle between life and death. Eventually, I couldn't stand anymore and I started to cut myself where not too much of damage could be done. For example, my arm, my legs and my fingers. Physical pain decreased the amount of my mental pain. But it didn't last long. Gradually, this turned [into] a cycle.

Finally, I began seeing a therapist who constantly talked to me about my problem and assured me that everything I tell her remains confidential, unless of course, I have the attempt to hurt myself again. Therapy didn't help too much at first. I started to read through the bible. Many passages touched me. From then on, every time when I struggle through the pains, I would pray to god, not for him to stop it immediately, but for him to get through that rough time with me, and he did. The pain lessened. I gotten better with God by my side and the help of the therapist. I grew stronger afterwards. I didn't blame God for putting all those pains on me. But rather, I thanked him in the end. If I never gone through something like that, I wouldn't have understood the pain, the misery and the struggle. Now that I understand, I can use it to help others who are going through similar problems.

God will always be my "idol", my dearest love, and the most power ruler of all. He loves me, just as he loves everyone else in this world. He will always be there to help me, guide me and lead me to the destiny that I'm chosen to follow.

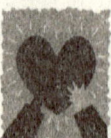

Tara

Did your family influence you to believe in God?
Well actually, yes they have, because I feel like they don't love me, they don't like me. So I feel the only person that does love me is God. Its not actually a person it's a spirit, but I feel that its the only thing, the only feeling I have is that He loves me. And at least I know He loves me.

How do you feel that God loves you since you say He's a spirit?
I can feel Him inside of me. I know He is inside of me. It's a warm feeling. Like a welcome feeling that He gives me.

Has He shown you in anyway in your life experience?
Well, yeah. He has never really given me a really big sign. He gave me little sign that He's there. Something like not too big. I'll be like, "God, why doesn't anyone love me?" And then my grandfather would call and say, "Hey, Tara I love you." So that's how I know He's around listening to me.

Do you talk to God a lot?
Yes, everyday, every night. Whenever I am mad, sad, stressed, or depressed.

Do you talk to people about God?
Sometimes. It depends on the person. Like if the person doesn't believe in God, I respect them and I don't speak about Him. But I try to convince them there is a God. And if they get defensive, then I just don't talk about God in front of them.

If I do not believe in God what would you say to convince me to believe in God?
Well to convince you, I would say…how did the plants get here, how did the earth, the dinosaurs…how are you living, if there is no God. I would convince them that way. If I get into it, I would tell you more. But right now I am not really thinking, thinking. But I would get into it and would say a whole bunch of things that comes out of no where.

What about people who believe in science? Like earth's evolution? Or Darwin's Law that God did not create man. What will be your argument?
I'm the type of person if people want to think that they can think that, but I won't think that. I will believe in it. They can believe whatever they want. My argument is that how can you say there is no God if you go through all these good things. Everybody has bad things and good things in their life. But there's a reason for those bad things to happen. So there is a reason for everything to happen. And I believe that God did that for a reason.

If you were to convince me to be a Christian what would be one testimony that you would tell me about your own life situation or experiences you had that there is a God?
My aunt's friend, well, he got hit by a truck and I prayed every night and everyday. And he died at first, but a couple of hours later he was alive. God brought him back to life. I felt like God did that.

Laura   18yrs

Q.   I well I wouldn't call it a religion,
~~I am a christian if you want~~
but I am a christian if you want a
@ name.

I was introduced to the church
once before and was intrigued by the
different races and the friendliness of the
people. But it was an event called womans
day at madison square guarden that
changed my life for the better. My
family ~~did~~ are not the church type people
and had no influence in my becoming
a disciple., It was totally new for me.

having a relationship with God
and being baptized as a follower of
Jesus Christ has changed my life in
numerous ways. I am not a the hateful
person I was, cursing and hating
everyone, carrying so much hate that I
once even dreamed of bombing my school.
I now ~~understand~~ beginning to understand
the true meaning of love and compassion.
I was a bitter person and suffered
from depression, most of my days now
I am joyful because I knew the truth and

because I believe I have found God's kingdom on earth - the church. I was lonely and had never known the meaning of true friend- ship, but now I am beginning to believe their is a such thing.

If you are a nonbeliever I tell you, nothing in all this earth, not money, guys or girls, sex, drugs, or riches is above God. No matter what you turn to & God is alive and you can't avoid him. Sooner or later you will have to encounter him whether you want to or not. Yes this world is corrupt and there's a lot of evils in this world but God does these things so that in your despair you can turn to him who is wise and true, knows you, and loves you too.

Yes it is very hard to be a Christian especially in this perverse generation we are in. It is difficult to love your enemies and put your trust and worries on God. Yes, sometimes I feel judged and many times persecuted. but I rejoice and am glad when I am

judged and persecuted because, you know
what Jesus went throughe it also,
and I rejoice because it is worth it.
when I teach

My dreams as a disciple......
wow! there are so many. well my
main dream is that I can become the
wise woman for God to impact so
many people's lives and baptize so
many people, possibly more than half
of the world. I dream of leading
and preaching in the church and travelling
many places doing God's work. I dream
of finding my soulmate in the church
and that we can lead together, having a
beutiful family and home. I dream of
finding a career in singing, acting, and
dancing all three, and that I can use
these talents in the church to inspire
people. I dream of writing my own songs
and getting many cd's made
from the songs.

Relationships,

Sex,

Pregnancy,

ProLife,

and

Adoption

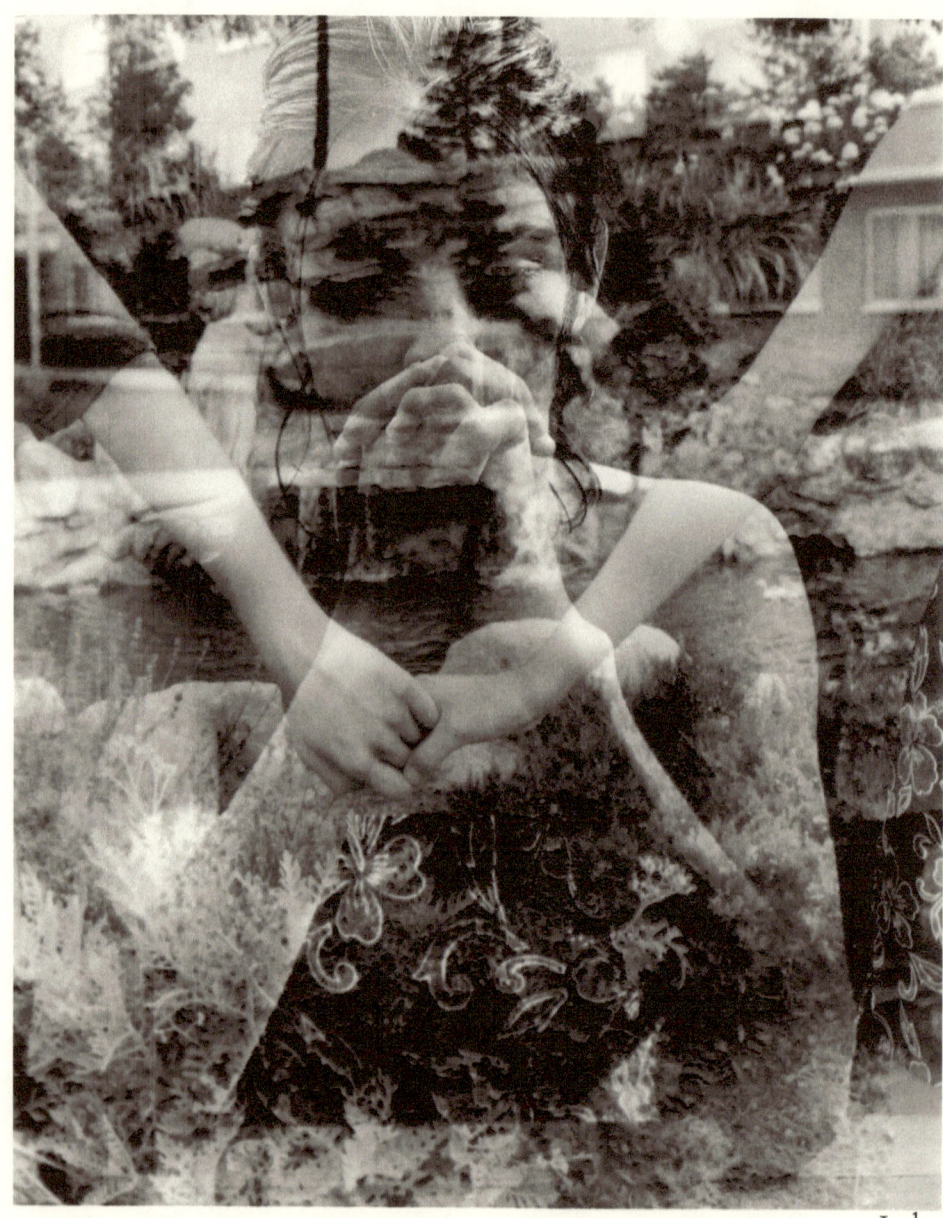

Jacky

Jacky

Tell me your best moment at summer college.
Well there are a lot of good ones. I have to say the best one was meeting Jorge.

Tell me about him.
Well, lets see. We meet the second or third day we were here and I remembered he befriended me when I sat by myself at lunch and he came over and sat with me, because he knew me from art class. We started talking and that day I had some trouble in the computer lab cause I don't know anything about computers so he stayed after and helped me. He waited for me to be done and then he walked me back to my room and we hung out and that's where it all started.

Where is he from?
Puerto Rico

And where are you from?
New Jersey

Woah, so when you guys leave are you going to continue this relationship?
Well, he still wants to. I really am in love, I won't deny it. But I have my doubts about it last week and I question him about it all the time. Cause it really worries me. Cause there is always that stereotype about guys who swear the world to the girl and then they go off with somebody else and forgets all about the other girl. And that's my biggest fear, but he swears that it won't happen and he never felt this way. So I hope I can take his word for it. I hope we can keep in contact and keep things going good.

Do you believe that he's keeping his word?
Well, there is only so much you could believe when you only know somebody for six weeks. But he seems very sincere. He doesn't even look at other girls. He's very, very good to me and very protective of me from other guys. So I really think he does care about me.

How do you feel about him being protective over you and how is he being protective over you?
Well sometimes he can get very territorial. When I'm hanging out with a guy he'll get kind of jealous and he'll come over and say, "Yo, what's going on?" or something. Or he would get back at me by purposely go flirting with other girls in front of me stuff like that.

How does that make you feel?

Well part of me, I feel kind of annoyed. That means that he doesn't trusted me so much or maybe thinks I'm weak that I can't stand up for myself. But then part of me thinks he is really sweet, because he doesn't want other guys near me.

So you guys are going to be separated from each other, how are you guys going to keep in contact?

Well he wants to do it by buying phone cards and email. He also has an aunt that lives up at Syracuse and he visits her once in a while. So when he sees her, he wants to come down to see me. He was talking to his mom about trying talking to my mom into letting me go on a trip down to Puerto Rico.

Wow, sound so serious.

Yeah, and also we both are in the same program, which is art, and he was talking about going to the same college as me so we can stay together after this year is over.

Do you believe in that? That you guys will be together in college?

Well, I tell him all the time that I am very understanding that he wants to see other people and just remain friends. I totally understand that. I rather not lose him as a friend, because I enjoy being with him and he saids the same thing to me. But he said, "No, no, no, I swear to you that we will still be together. And I really, really love you." I hope he means it. I think maybe right now he thinks he does, but I have a gut feeling when he gets home, he's probably going to forget about me. But I don't want that to happen I still want us to be friends.

What do you think about people who just jump into relationships, because we are only here for six weeks. You had a relationship within two days or something?

Well, I first started become friends with him on the second day we were here and then about a week later we actually started liking each other.

Do you feel like you just jumped into the relationship?

Sort of and sort of not. I feel like I jumped into it, because a week long is not enough to get to know someone. On the other hand we are only here for six weeks. I don't think we were really rush into it, but I think we kinda were.

If you were to go back what would you change?
What would I change? Um... You know what, I don't really regret anything. I'm glad I met somebody like him. Cause I never met anybody who ever cared about me this much. Ever. Nobody ever cared about me this much. Wants to spend as much time with me in my life. This is pretty good.

How does this make you feel?
It makes me feel special. It makes me feel wanted. I never felt like this before. Every other guy I had, had been you know what I mean... I'm not saying all my other boyfriends were jerks. I would never do that. They had their moments. But none of them has cared for me like this. Like you couldn't even compare it.

How do you see your future with him?
Well, its kinda hard to say right now. I guest I have to wait for a little while after this is over to determine whether we can still make it or not. But as of right now, I think we do still feel strongly about each other. I feel strongly about him anyway. I hope we will keep the momentum going. Hopefully, we'll go off to the same college together and maybe even just be friends if the relationship doesn't work out. That's all I want.

4/23/01
Amy
18 years old.

At the very young age of 15, I started dating older men. And not older like 17 or 18, it was more like 25.

I think that the whole driving force behind me wanting to date older men was that I was already extremly mature. And I know that sounds extremly selfish and self-centered, but I'm not trying to be. All I'm saying is that guys my age then (and now) were always kind of beneath my intelligence. But I do have an age limit. I will NEVER, EVER date anyone who is 20 years older than me. EVER.

I think that since I am pretty mature, I didn't need any man to make me feel that way. And I don't think I EVER will.

There are some pretty big differences between dating guys my age and (→)

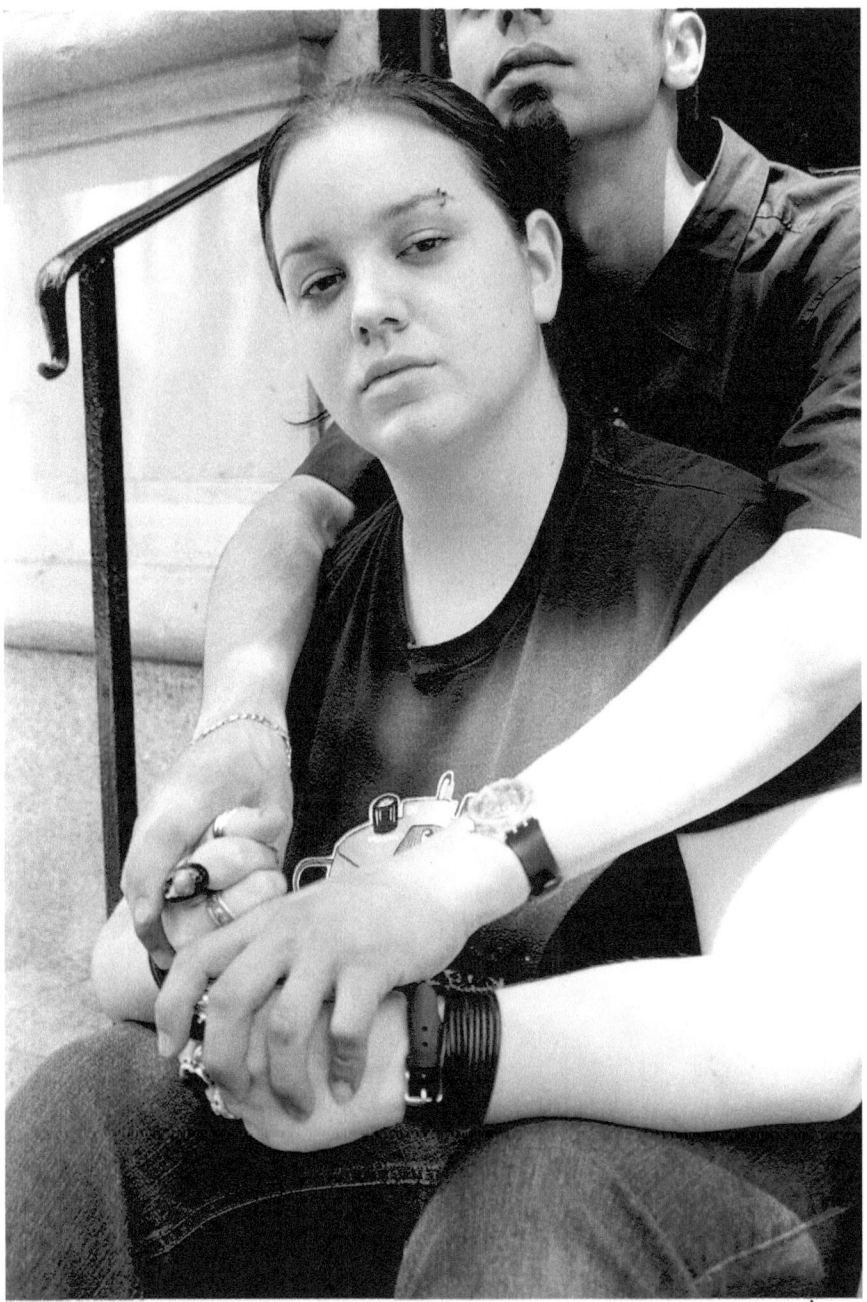

Amy

older guys. For instance, a younger guy will make fun of you, an older guy will joke with you. A younger guy will almost always try to make any private time with them into a sexual situation. An older guy will just want to hold you. If things reach a sexual level during that period of time, its because you [BOTH] wanted it not because anybody felt pressured into anything.

One wonderful experience I had with my boyfriend when I was 15 was just driving around Manhattan. It was a lot of fun because we walked talk and just basically. The one bad experience was when he told me that I was the other women, that he already had a girlfriend that he was on and off with and that he was dumping me for her. It really hurt and jaded me.

Well, this particular guy I just basically bumped into and we saw each (=)

other and dug each other. We exchanged
phone numbers and the next thing
you knew we were dating.

And yes, it is a little scary to
hook up with a stranger. But not
just older men, men in general.
You don't know how their mind works.
One day you could think that their
cool and normal and the next day
they could seriously hurt you. Mentally,
Physically, emotionally. Or the feelings
you develop for them could
be scary. You might actually
start to open yourself, let them, and
fall in love. But its not just older
men, its all guys.

In my case, I've been very lucky.
I haven't encountered anyone who was
twisted. No one's ever stalked me and
no one has ever caused me any
physical harm.

My parents have always been
very liberal. I've never really had ☺

hide my relationships from them. They knew that I am pretty intelligent and that I am a pretty good judge of character. They know that if I am dating someone, that they can trust me. My current boyfriend is 29, soon to be 30. My parents know, and at first gave a protective raise of an eyebrow, but knew (and know) that they can trust me.

I have never dated just to get attention. The only reason that I've dated anyone was because I've felt strongly about them. Sure, someone opening doors for you and saying they like the way you smell is wonderful! But girls who only date for the attention have a lack of love for themselves. And it's really sad.

If I ever have a daughter, yes, I would let her date older men. I hate hypocrites, so why would I be one myself? Also, I would like ⇒

to think that my daughter would be intelligent, and I would always trust her to make the right choices.

The advice that I have to give to any other teenage girls about dating older men is just to trust yourself before trusting anybody else. And if you feel that you have to hide it from your parents, then something is wrong with the relationship.

Dating, in general, can be a wonderful thing. Especially if you find that certain someone with whom you connect on so many different levels. I'm one of the lucky ones because I believe that I've found that, and yes, in an older man.

Mauricia 16

When did you two first get together?

Okay, so, we had a job at a camp, Hidden Valley, over the summer. It was kind of twisted and complicated. We were both doing different things. When I first met him it was like, I liked him, but he looked kind of old. I didn't think he would go for me. So, I was like, ok fine, he's not for me and I kind of dealt with that. Because I didn't feel at the time he would perceive me as his type and I wasn't sure. So we kind of remain as friends. And I used to talk this other guy and his name was *Gary and we used to mess around and he was a real ass like he was like a asshole. Well one day, Kyle finally came up to me. He was like, "You know what, can you meet me tonight at 10:30pm in front of the cafeteria." And I was like, "O my god, can this be it?" Because you know its true, now when I talk him, all this time he was hinting me that he did liked me. But I didn't know if he was hinting that he did like me or him just being friendly, because he's very friendly. So when he asked me to meet him at 10:30pm in from of the cafeteria, now…, that's the spot where everybody is like, "O (Moan) give me some baby." So I was like, (Grasp) "OK," I was all nervous. So I met him, and umm, he brought me some cookies cause I told him I wanted some cookies and umm. We started talking and it was kind of strange, because it was just us sitting there. And it was so romantic cause we're outside and you have the open view of the beautiful sky. And you know upstate New York is like no pollution and you can actually see all the stars and there were a lot of shooting stars and stuff. We just started talking about everything. That's one thing I love about him, that we could talk about any and everything. So we were just talking and talking and talking. And in my head I'm like, "O my god, do something." There was that dead silence when nobody was saying anything and that was strange and he finally said, "Is it ok if I kiss you." And I was like, (Grasp) "O my god." And then I was like, "Do you think I would say no?" and he was like, "Well, I just wanted to know if it's alright with you?" And I was like "Yeah." And so we were kissing and it was like beautiful. Just beautiful. And it went from that innocent sweet fresh first kiss to that hot passionate sexy, "O take my clothes off baby." Kind of kiss. It was really nice. We are on the grass now, and then the deers came and nearly trample our heads. That was kind of a cue to go away. From that day, we started talking and we weren't just friends anymore, but something more. So that's how we first met.

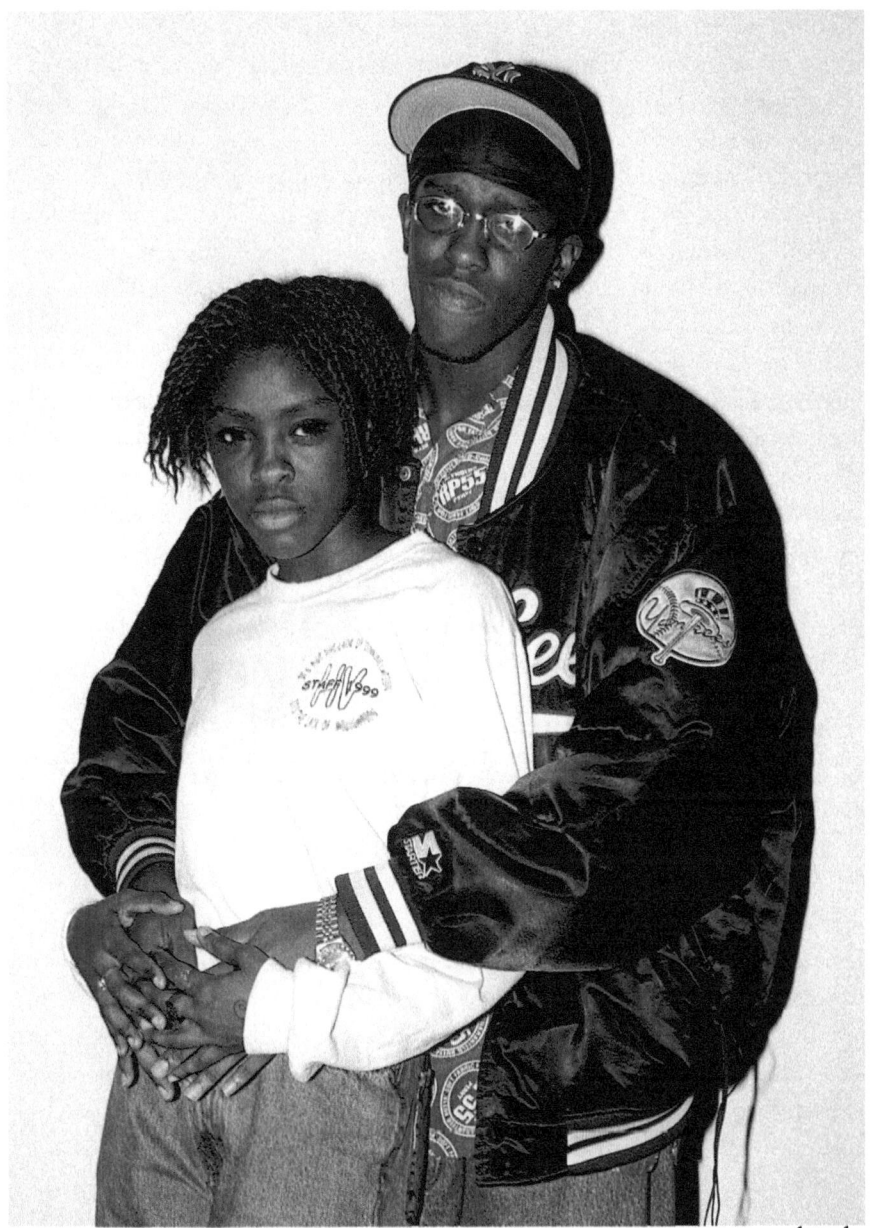

Mauricia and Kyle

Now that you're back in the city, is it difficult for guys you to see each other?
O yes, its much difficult now. Cause when we were back at the camp we saw each other everyday. Like every second cause we were in this close community type environment. And now that we are back in the city, he lives in the Bronx and I live in Brooklyn. And we have to kind of sneak and creep around, because my mother is a real bitch and she won't let me see him. I call him in the middle of the night. I would be like, (Whisper) "Psst, hello." And I think he is real nice about it. And I kind of figure he's 18 and I'm 16. He doesn't have a lot of rules to live by. And I asked him before, "Why are you still with me when you could be with some other girl who if you want to see her, you could see her." He was like, "You're special and I love you." So I was like ok, that's really nice. But its really hard, because I don't see him as much as I want to and as much as we used to. But we still have that thing. We make the best of what we have right now and we are just wait for that day when we don't have to be so seclusive and sneaky. We can just show our... like run naked in the streets or something. I don't know how to explain it. When I finally have that freedom and be like, "Mom, I'm gonna see Kyle." And not like "Mom, um, I'm going out with Anna and Flonia to the library." So we are just waiting for that day.

So you can trust this guy?
O yes, I can trust him. He's a real sweetheart. I know him from before we even went out. I knew him just as a friend. Like a friend you wanted and his personality, he's not a person that cheats. He hates that and he said he has friends that cheats on their girlfriend and he can't stand that, because if he was in a relationship, he wants his partner to be just as loyal as he is. And if he finds that the relationship is going sour or not quite where it should be, and its not working out, there's no use in just cheating on the person and hurting their feelings. When you can just say, "This is not working out and I think we should move on." End it like that. Instead of cheating and messing around and hurting feelings and all those things. So I know he's not that type of person. And I could trust him.

Do see a future with him?
Yeah, I see a future with him. I don't know how to explain it, there is something that keeps us together. Like some glue, some sticky stuff that's making me want to stay with him and nobody else. Like feelings that were never felt before are being felt. Its just like magical. If anything, lets just say that it doesn't work

out the way I want to and we do go our separate ways, he's not the person that I would say, "Dam, why did I ever go out with him." I could not see myself saying that he just wasted my time. Because whatever we do together its just special. It always keep a special place in my heart. When he said corny stupid line and I'm like "Illll." But its just sweet, because it's a little corny stupid line. He always looks out for my best interests. Like for some guys they want sex. Sex, sex, sex, sex. And I know for a fact that Kyle is not a virgin. And I'm not going to hold that against him, because the past is the past and what happened, happened. Sex is not like a problem. Because some boys or some couples feel that they must have sex to keep a relationship and that's not a problem with me, because we had like many opportunities or places that we could have like fuck each other minds out and that was not even the case. We were doing stuff that it could have came to that point and we could have done it and I just said, "No, I'm not ready for this." And he didn't get like, "O, I cannot believe you." He was always really sweet, kind, and gentle. And lets just say we reach a point where we are about to have sex, and I said, "You know what, I'm not ready." He didn't blow up in my face. He would just hold me sometimes and I just love to cuddle. He's not afraid to cuddle.

Sounds like he has respect for you.
Yes, he has a lot of respect for me. He always talking about me. When I call his house, his grandmother, "O missy (Mauricia's nickname), ..." and his five-year-old sister would be like, "Mmm, Kyle's girlfriend." And all of that its just a nice warm feeling.

What do you like most about him?
Our friendship. Our trust. The fact that we are in two separate world, but when our world meet they don't like crash and burn. We just kinda fuse them together and just make this one big beautiful world kind of thing. We can talk about anything or everything and there's no insecurity about "O, I don't think I could ever tell him this." Sometimes, I would be feeling something and I don't want to tell him, he would always picks it up. He would be like, "Ahh, what's wrong with you, you could tell me." And he helps me whenever I needed help. He was always there to help me and cope with my craziness and he can make me laugh even though I make him laugh more, because I'm Mauricia, and I'm just crazy like that. He just knows how to make me feel better and touch me on the right spot.

Young Sisters

Yeah?
Yeah (Laughs)

Now that you experience this with your mother's relationship for her not allowing you to have a boyfriend. What would you do if you're a mother, would you allow your daughter to go out and date at your age, at sixteen?
I think at age sixteen, you should be mature enough to go out and date. And I said this before, I would let my daughter date at sixteen and if I felt that she is mature enough at fourteen, sure I will let her date, because the simple fact is that if you don't let them, they will do it anyway. And that's the way it is. I would rather her do it, not "it," but date with me knowing and that she's dating and I know the guy and I know where she is. Than her sneaking around going behind my back, I think she's one place and she's not. So I would like everything to be on the floor, on the table, and *I will establish that relationship with my kid, that they could come and could tell me everything and how they're feeling. And they don't have to go to somebody else when they should be coming to me.* And that's one thing that I don't like in the relationship with my mother. Cause I can't tell her how I feel and everything has to be behind her back and that's not healthy.

So I would let her date. I hate that stupid double standard that boys could date at six and girls have to date at like sixteen or like thirty-one. So these six-year-old boys that could date their parents are like, "Yeah, my little Billy is dating." And the girl, "O, Susie, no, Susie has to stay inside." And so it always end up the girls is sneaking around, because no matter what, she never has permission to go out and I hate that. So I would want to establish that relationship, "Yes, you can date, but I want to know where you are. And if you are going out with Tommy, tell me that you are going out with Tommy don't say that you are going by your friend's house, because I will find out. I mean I may not find out right away, but I will find out. So just let me know where are you going and let me know. I won't hold you for it, because these are feelings that you are going to feel. If you are going to raise a child right enough to know right from wrong. You should have it in your heart to say, "You know what I am going to send my son or daughter out into that world," because these are feelings that you can't contain.

Aisha and Judith

Hey what's up my name is Aisha and I'm Judith and **we're proud virgins.**

Whoa you guys are virgins?
Yeah.

Are a lot of your friends virgins?
No.

Why are you guys proud to be virgins then?
Well I'm proud to be a virgin, because I think it takes a lot to remain a virgin now a days especially being that I'm almost reaching adulthood, I'm eighteen-years-old, I'm going to college and all of my other friends have lost their virginity already. And I remain a virgin, because I have a strong will and I decided that I'm going to do what I have to do and sex is not part of it right now..

Now that you are talking about being a virgin, it seem like you are a survivor, like "O my gosh I survive being a virgin." How do you feel about having your peers being non-virgins who are always talking about sex and the media constantly having a sexual image of teenagers in your face. Do you feel pressure by that?
I don't because, just because you are a virgin it doesn't mean you can't speak about sex with your friends that are not a virgin, you know. You see it on TV, it doesn't mean that "I saw that hot passion thing, I'm going to going to do it cause I'm a freak." No, you just do whatever you want, you know. Just because you decided to be a virgin doesn't mean you can't do other things, but that's a whole other subject.
I don't really feel pressure, because I don't think I'm in love and I don't think having sex is love. I think they are two different things. Sex is one thing and making love is another. Being in love is a completely different thing and I am in love without having sex. So I don't feel pressure by everybody else. I mean everybody talks about it and you know I see my friends and I see it on TV. But I have something that's mine in my heart. That I know I can be in love without all the added pressure and stress of having sex.

Have you ever been pressure by your boyfriends on having sex?
Ahhh, one occasion with one guy. This one guy I dated in ninth grade, it was always like an issue for him. We eventually broke up, not really because of that. But you know, that was one of the issue that we broke up.

Do you talk to your parents about sex?
No.

Do you feel like that is an issue for teens that they don't talk to their parents about sex? Or parents don't want to talk to their teens about sex?
I think that in different ethnic families, its different, because in our family sex is like, "Don't talk about sex." That just not acceptable. But in other ethnic families, sex is an open subject to everybody and young as three and as big as twenty-five, its not a taboo like I have in my family.
Right, like in my family we talk about sex, not like it's an open discussion at the dinner table. But it's not a problem for me to go to my mother and ask her a question about something sexual. Like when I was little my mother would take me to Victoria Secret with her and say, "Look at what lingerie I'm buying." And I guess that I know so much it made me not want to go that way. I know how things can be, I know the pressures. So because of the knowledge I have, it made me not want to do it.

Do you feel other people who don't have the knowledge about sex they go off doing it, because they want that experience, they want that excitement?
Not necessary, because I know someone who did know about sex and all the consequences, know all the bad things, and ended up having sex and getting pregnant before entering high school and having a kid. So you know, it's your own choice. If you decide to have sex regardless whether you are aware of the choices or not. That's a big problem.

Do you encourage your friends to stay being a virgin or not to have sex?
Umm, well Judith being friend. I find that I don't have to influence her and encourage her because she can make her own decision about herself. You know what is right for you and what's wrong for you. For me that's not right. For her it might be right at anytime, but right now its not the right time for her either. But I don't feel like I need to encourage her or discourage her.

Now having sex is about life or death because of virus such as, AIDS and all these STDs. Do you think that have a greater impact on you to stay a virgin and not to have sex?

Yeah, its scary if you think about it, just because you have sexual contact with one person you could have the rest of your life effected by that you know. And who wants that really? Nobody, so you just stay away from what you don't want.

I had a friend who really gave her heart and soul to this guy and she lost her virginity to him. She thought they had a special relationship between them and she found out that he was cheating on her. And the girl he cheated on her with had herpes. And herpes is incurable. She was afraid that she had herpes. When she told me about that story it made me think. You never know no matter how secure you are. You never know.

Do you think being a virgin is a really big thing for a girl and even to give it up to a guy?

Yeah, cause its something you prize. If you have a ring that belongs to your great grandmother, you wouldn't want to give it to just anybody. You give it to someone special and if you don't feel like that person is special enough, then why give it.

Do you have anything to add on this issue being a virgin?

I think everyone should be a virgin until they are eighteen or an adult, because they don't know how to take care of themselves let alone taking care of themselves having sex, because they get caught up in the heat of the moment and they forget all the other consequences that could happen. It happens to adults too you know, but I'm saying if you're still in high school, why put yourself through all these other stresses of having sex. You have enough stress already.

I personally feel that there is more to my life than just having sex in relationships or sexual relationships. There are so many other things you can explore and learn about that person inside and out without having sex with that person. So I think that's the end of everything. Its not the end of a relationship is the sexual experience. I feel like I am going to wait until I get married, because of the belief I have. And because of respect for my parents, especially my mother, because my mother ask me to wait. Like this ring I have, this is a waiting ring that my mother gave me. And I'm going to wait. That's what I'm going to do. I respect her and my belief.

So that ring symbolizes your commitment to wait for that right person, to get married and then have sex.
Yeah.

Do you think being a virgin is not cool anymore or that's what other teens think and you don't follow that, you don't join that club?
I think being virgin is the best thing, because you don't fall into a number of categories of most high school girls. You know that 90% of the student body isn't a virgin. There's just that few percent that have decided to wait because there's no point in giving it up to someone who you know you will not be with for the rest of your life. They might be serious with you at that moment, but after that, what happen? You are a kid, you have so many other things to do. I just think that being a virgin is the best thing.
I believe being a virgin is the best thing. And it doesn't matter to me, it doesn't matter what's cool, because I feel like I am different. I grew up different from other people. And other people may not see what's normal to them or what they would think is cool, but I don't really care you know. That is something that I hold for myself. This is right for me and how everyone else feel doesn't affect me.

Before we end is there anything else you want to speak out to girls who are out there thinking about being a virgin or not. What would be your advice to them?
I would have to say as a person, I can't judge them, because I don't know what is going on in their lives. Because they may make a decision to stay a virgin or not, but just make sure whatever they do not to regret it. If you are going to do something don't regret doing it, because that's the worst feeling, when you regret something.
And like people always say listen to your heart and I believe you shouldn't listen to your heart. Because sometimes you can get caught up in the heat and emotions and passion and stuff like that. And instead its been said your heart is easily wicked, you know. And who can really know your heart? Don't listen to your heart listen to what your mind saids, logically what's right, and whats wrong before doing anything. And when you know at that time is not the right time then don't do it.

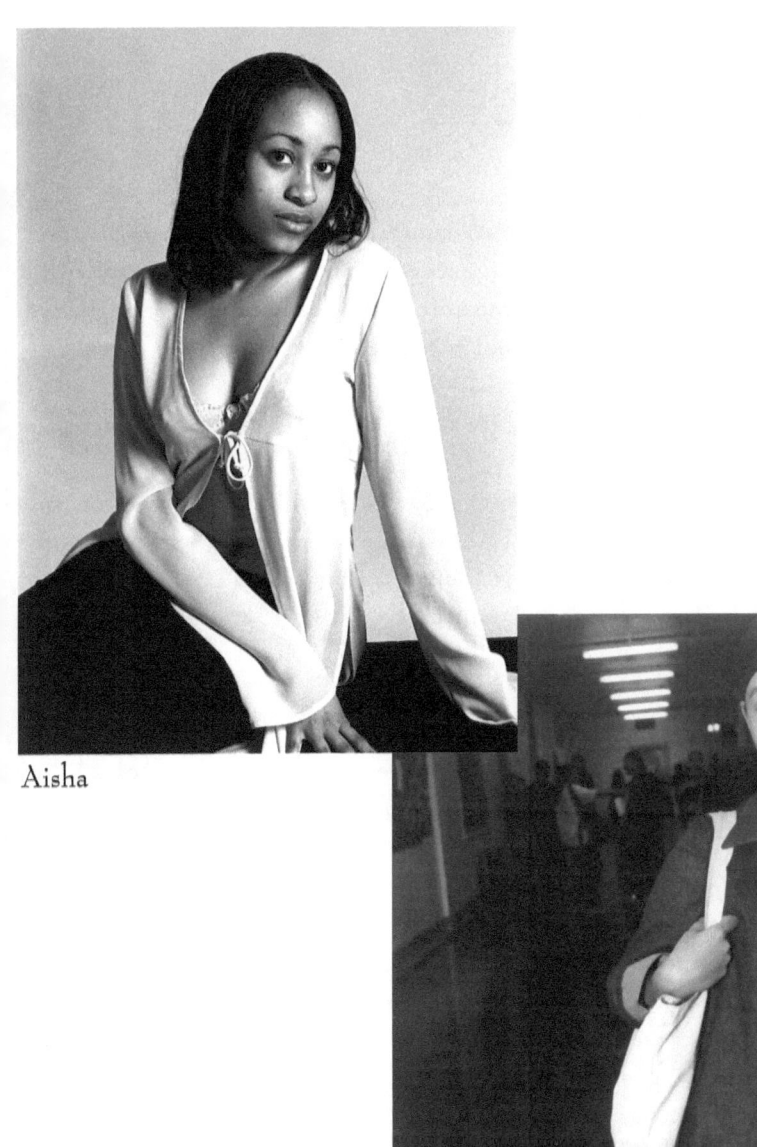

Aisha

Judith

Shenell

How old were you when you first had sex?
Fifteen.

Did you talk about it before you had sex? Such as birth control that you were going to use?
I didn't really talk about birth control, because I really wasn't concern with it at the time. I was only in the ninth grade. It wasn't planned. It just happened. In a way, I regret it and in a way I don't regret it.

What were the reasons why you had sex? Was it peer pressure, the media, or you just wanted to do it, and there was no outside influence?
No, I mean, I think that not even about peer pressure, but there were outside influence. Cause my girlfriends were having sex also and they would come with their stories. And I would hear them. As far as I'm concern, I'm not a follower and I had sex, because I wanted to have sex and sex feels good. (Laughing)

Did you trust your partner when you had sex with him?
Yeah, I trusted him. But then, I shouldn't have trust him, because of a lot of things I found out afterwards. That he was a *dog* and stuff like that.

What do you mean that he was a dog?
He used to talk to other girls. Stuff like that. I don't know if he was fucking other girls, but he's a *dog*.

What are some of the consequences you are thinking now after having sex? Like, "O, I might get pregnant, I might get a disease."
I mean I think about those consequences. That's why I take the shot so I can't get pregnant. And as far as diseases, I've never contracted a STD. Thank God. God forbid if I ever do. Um, I just take it day by day. The guy I am with now, I trust him a lot. We're about to be blah, blah, blah years. I've never received anything from him and I don't plan on it and if I ever do, I know who's it from.

Did you have an AIDS test before you had sex with this partner?
No.

So you trust your partner?
Yes, but I have one afterwards though.

Why?
Just to have one afterwards. When I went to have a GYN, they did everything. So I had one. Even though it was kind of scary. Even though I know I don't have that shit. But, you know, just to be on the safe side.

What were some of your expectations before having sex?
Like what they do on the movies? (Loud Laugh) **But it wasn't!** Um... it was like fifteen minutes. It was so whack. It was Sooooo WHACK. **IT WAS MAD WHACK.** (Loud Laugh again) And thats why I wish that the guy I am with now, that I gave my virginity to him, because believe me, if anybody is listening to this tape and if you're a virgin, do not give these mother fuckers out here. DO NOT GIVE IT TO THEM. **Wait**, wait, as long as you can. Cause in the long run it will be really, really special. If I can be a virgin again, I would be a virgin again.

Anything to add?
Um...ABSTANINCE! **Is the best thing to do.** But if you are going to have sex, please make sure you take the right preventions. You take contraception so you don't get pregnant. Or you go and get a GYN, just to check your private parts. To make sure everything is intact, that everything is okay. So that you don't have to say, "Dam, I should have known." Because you do know, there are a lot of information, there's the media, there's friends you can talk to and get information from.

Young Sisters

Bernice

1) How old were you when you got pregnant?
2) Did you use any type of protection? Who's decision was it?
3) What was going on in your head when you realized you were pregnant?
4) Did your boyfriend reject you when he found out that you were pregnant?
5) How long did your relationship last after your pregnancy?
6) What kind of treatment did you get from the public, peers, teachers, and family?
7) Did you think about abortion?
8) Is your boyfriend trying to get custody of the child?
9) Has your boyfriend supported you during your pregnancy?
10) How do you support your baby, when you go to school? Where does your baby go?
11) What is a typical day for you?
12) What are your hopes and dreams for your baby now?

1. I was 16 years old.

2. condoms. my decision

3. sadness, tiredness, scared for my baby.
4. for the safety

4. No.

5. 2 yrs. & 2 months. all together.

6. Everyone was happy and sad.

Dirty looks and rejection from teacher

7. No don't believe in them.

8 No, he don't care

9. yes all throughout the pregnancy.

10. I work, I stay out of school some times. She goes to the first Steps Daycare

11. wake up at 6:30 dress myself and the baby. Baby's father comes to pick us up. come drop the baby off at daycare. and go to classes. Go home and chill

12. I want her to do good. and become big.

Bernice
Deelilah.   18

-76-

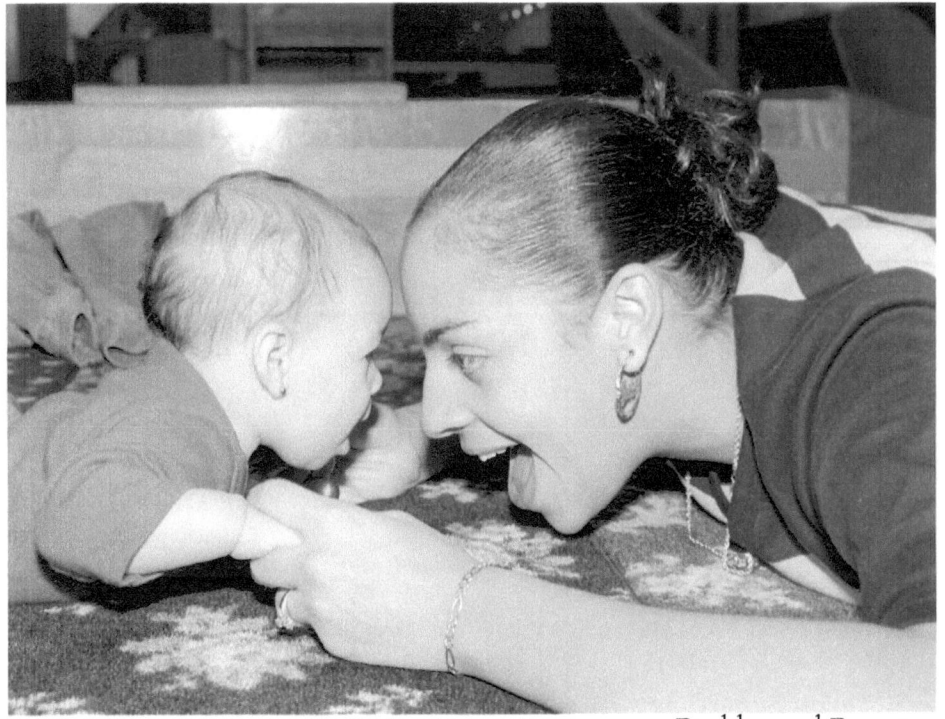

Deelilan and Berenice

1) When I got pregnant me along w/ my family were all in shock. My mother not so much, she said she had a feeling about it. It made me feel strange and unprepared. But I got used to the idea.

2) The whole process birth was painful but Relieving. The contractions are the worst. The responsibility you get is tremendous. This is because you feel strange about taking care of yourself and a baby.

3) Being a teenage mom is not easy. I feel so strange sometimes when I say "my daughter". Sometimes when you look at the both of you in the mirror it feels more like ~~the~~ your little brother or sister. I'm grateful for having because ~~a~~ the baby brings you so much joy and happiness. Sometimes

you may get depressed by the thought but then you look at your baby and you feel ~~so~~ better.

Jenna and *Leslie*

I don't know what I would do if I got pregnant at sixteen and I would be so scared. *You know things happen for a reason. I can sit here and say that I would not have an abortion. But if I were in that situation, that would be the first thing that will come in my mind. Because I don't want to deal with it you know. But then, right now, its so cool, because there are so many other things you can do. Like you can have the baby, go to the hospital and give it to them no questions asked, just hand it over.* In New York City, we have high schools with teenage mothers coming into school with their babies. We have this program for teenage mom to drop off their baby and the center will take care of it and when they are done with school they come and pick them up.

But when you go right down to the core of it, its society's fault, because they promote it a lot on T.V. They don't tell how people can prevent pregnancy from happening. *At what age were you guys taught about reproduction and abstinence?* Ummm, I would say twelve or thirteen. *Twelve? Why don't they do it in high school?* And then in high school they teach you about your cervix instead of how to use a condom. These things are inside they're important to know about, but what about having children.

And if you are, there are so many things you can use. I mean you can't depend on the condom. Cause the condom is not a 100%. It could break. You can't trust a guy. If he say he's gonna pull out, don't ever believe him. My friend was very, very sorry that she did. She didn't get pregnant, but she taught she was.

Another thing I don't like is how society makes a girl feel they have to be a certain way. Totally hate it. Society looks at sex as being cool, yet they treat girls who get pregnant like they are out cast. *Yeah, they are the sluts and whores?* Yeah, where is the responsibility? *Where are the guys? The guys have nothing.* The guys are cool, because they knocked up some girl. That's how they treat guys. *Girls are the one that end up with the baby. The one that end up paying everything.* The guys just don't care. *The guy just go humping somebody. Like somebody else.* Guys should get pregnant and see what its like. *Hey, you never know with the new technology.*

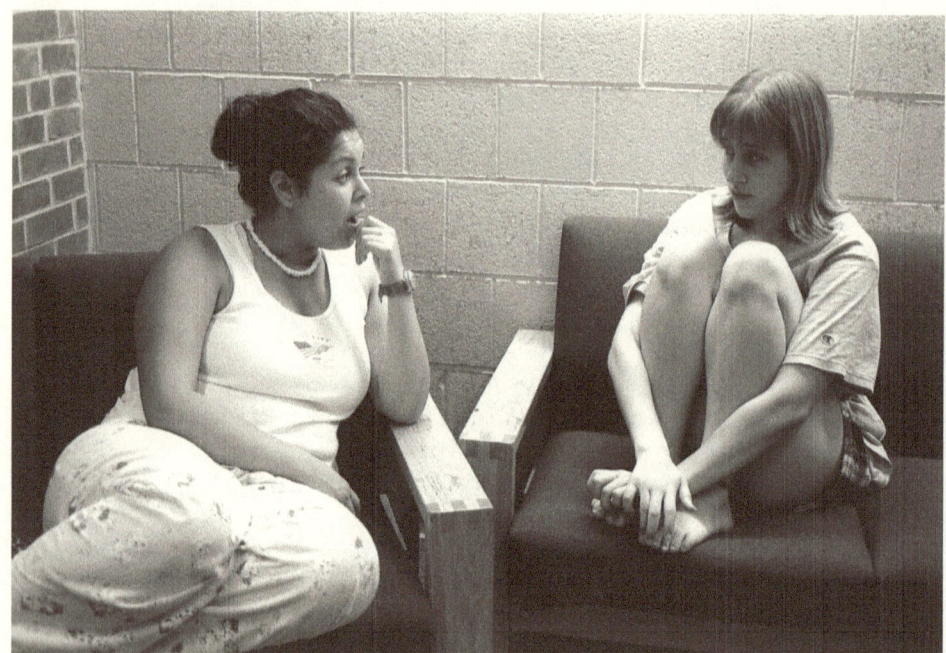

Leslie and Jenna

I think all schools should support abstinence. Instead of saying here's condoms. Its like you're promoting sex, when you are really suppose to prevent it.
And their is response are, "Well you know they are doing it anyways, so why not..."
They are like, if they are going to do it, they might as well do it safely and that's true. But people do it for the wrong reasons.

They should start with the little kids when they are young. Cause there eleven-year-olds and ten-year-olds doing it.
You see it on the Jenny Jones show with twelve-year-old girls who get pregnant. *You have twelve-year-olds that has like a stomach, come on. She had eleven years living in this world.*
Eleven years, you haven't experience anything. She's gonna lose out on all these experiences when she's a teenager, because she ruin her life and got pregnant.

You know what I believe in, those little automatic babies that act like babies. They should have that, instead of carrying around a flour bag.
Those are really good ideas. We had to carry them around for a week all day in school. They had a little program that beeps. It didn't cry, but it beeped in the middle of the night. We have to wake up and stick a bottle in its mouth. By the end of the week you just wanted to scream and throw it against the wall, because it drove you nuts. I babysat a lot for little babies. They're so cute, but they are such a hassle. You're not taking care of them, you're not the one who have to change their dippers, the one who is giving the bath, the one who is feeding, the one who is waking up two o'clock in the morning. *They are also so expensive.* Dippers and doctor visits, even when you are pregnant you have to get all that stuff, hospitals and you give birth.

Society is so messed up.
And all these people who are like, "Yeah, I lost my virginity, that's kinda cool." *Its also peer pressure. It has to do a lot with peer pressure.*
If you do it, even though you do it before marriage, people do it for the wrong reasons. They do it, because their friends are doing it and they do it, because someone is pressuring them. But you really need to love somebody, if you want to do that and you need to know that they love you back.

ProLife

I met these girls at my hotel during my stay in Washington DC. They were all Roman Catholic, from St. Louis, Missouri. They were in Washington DC for five days to participate in the ProLife march.

Lindsay 14. First time marching.
I am here to stand up for what I believe in and that is once a baby is conceive it has a life and it shouldn't be taken away. So many babies are being killed each year, that I think we need to stand up and do what we can to help. I wanted to get a message across that a baby's life is very important and it shouldn't be taken away just because the mother doesn't want to care for it.

Alison 14. First time marching.
I'm fighting for ProLife in Washington DC, because once a baby is conceive its life and you shouldn't murder anyone, if you murder a baby or committing murder to, so you be should be held against it and it should be illegal. It doesn't mean that after a baby is born its life, its once it's conceive its life. Abortion should be made illegal because, it doesn't matter how old or when you kill something, its that you are killing it.

Lisa 17.
I'm here in Washington DC for the ProLife march, because I believe that everybody has the right to life. No matter how old or how young. And just because somebody's mother or father believe they shouldn't be here, they still should have the right to be born.

Carolyn 18. Third time marching.
I'm here at Washington DC marching for ProLife to protect all human life. Not just for the unborn, but also the elderly, and anyone who is a human, but especially for the unborn babies though because for me as a person and as a Roman Catholic believe that a child is human once it is conceive. Cause there is nothing magical happen once it comes through the birth canal. Its born when its conceive by it's mother and father. Babies don't have a voice when they are in the womb to stand up and speak for themselves, to stand up for their own rights. I find it to be my job to do that for them.

What is ProLife?
That you support everyone having the right to live. Being supportive of all human life. Whether it's a child who hasn't been born yet, or a person that is elderly and living in a nursing home. Any type of person. A person is a person.

I think being ProLife means that you care about everyone and you want to stand up for all the little babies that don't have voices to speak. I think everyone who is ProLife is their job to stand up for the children, because they can't speak inside their mothers' wombs.

Are you proud to be part of ProLife?
Yes. (Everybody)

Why are you proud about being ProLife?
I feel that even by coming to Washington DC to march is a small part of what I can do for the unborn and all those who can't speak up for themselves. It's trying to do my part as I can.
I think its something that you believe in. Its something you hold strongly and dearly to yourself and you should be proud of the things you do.
I think its something you want to help people because you know there are so many babies that are being killed each year and that could be adopted. You just want to see their life keep going on.
I think that you respect all life. You should stand up to show that you respect it.

How did the ProLife march start?
I think this is the 23th anniversary of the decision called Roe vs. Wade.
When abortion was made legal.
It started the next year that people came to protest that Supreme Court could pass a law like this, that they disagree with it. They came to Washington to protest it and it just continue every year on the anniversary, which is January 22.
I think it continue for so long because people believe in it so very strong on this issue.

Do you think ProLife is working to fight against abortion?
I think some states have made it illegal, but I think for it to be successful the whole United States has to do it. So people can't go to other states to have an abortion and go back to their state that is illegal.
Every year it gets bigger too. Some reporter guy interview me for a local news station in St. Louis before we left. He asked me if we were doing any good coming and doing the march. And I said, "Of course." And he asked, "Is there an end to it? Do you see an end in sight?" and I said, "Well I would hope that this is the last year we would have to march and next year it would change." So I think if it keeps on getting big enough. People like us, the young kids who will be making decisions and voting to change it when we get old enough, I think it will end really soon.

What do you think of people get rape and want to have an abortion?
<u>I think that they could have the baby and put it up for an adoption. Just give
the baby a chance to live.</u>
I think that a lot of people would gladly adopt a child if they want to. There
are tons of people who are having an abortion when the baby could be adopted
by a loving family.
There are other alternatives than just abortion out there.
*Plus there is a saying "two wrongs don't make a right." Just because an violent act
was committed upon you, that you were rape and obviously that's horrible and to
carry a child from such a violent act would be even worst but to kill that child because
something harmful was done to you its not going to make it better, its just going to
make you feel worst. And plus the percentage of people who abort babies, because
they were rape is like 1% of all the 99% of non developed babies.*

*What happens if there is a pregnant mom, wants to have the baby, but can't support
it, what would you say to them?*
There are lots of families that I think would love to adopt the child into a
loving family. If the mother couldn't support the baby then another family
could provide what the baby needs.
<u>Also there's like reach out centers that will give you a... like our school has
a ProLife program they have a box that the parents can put in baby stuff that
you can give to mothers who cannot support their babies. So there's those stuff
out there too.</u>
*I think if the mother really knows that the baby is human life and she really wants to
carry it then she shouldn't have anyone influence her otherwise, because they don't
know how it is to be a mom they don't know how it feels to have that child inside
of you. She shouldn't let anybody else to convince her otherwise. Like they were
saying, there are tons of other options. There's tons of programs you can get into like
tell parents who want to adopt the child and they will pay for everything. Like the
medical bills and everything until you have the child and adopt the child after you deliver.*
**I definitely wouldn't say anything to discourage her from having a child,
just because of her situation, because there are so much help out there you
can get these days from other people.**

Does your school talk about ProLife?
*I think going to a catholic school it does but not a public school, it wouldn't. We go
to a private girls' catholic school in St Louis. I think this week while we're gone they
are having a ProLife speaker and ProLife week.*
In our school they have a ProLife club that meets every week we talk
about ProLife issues.

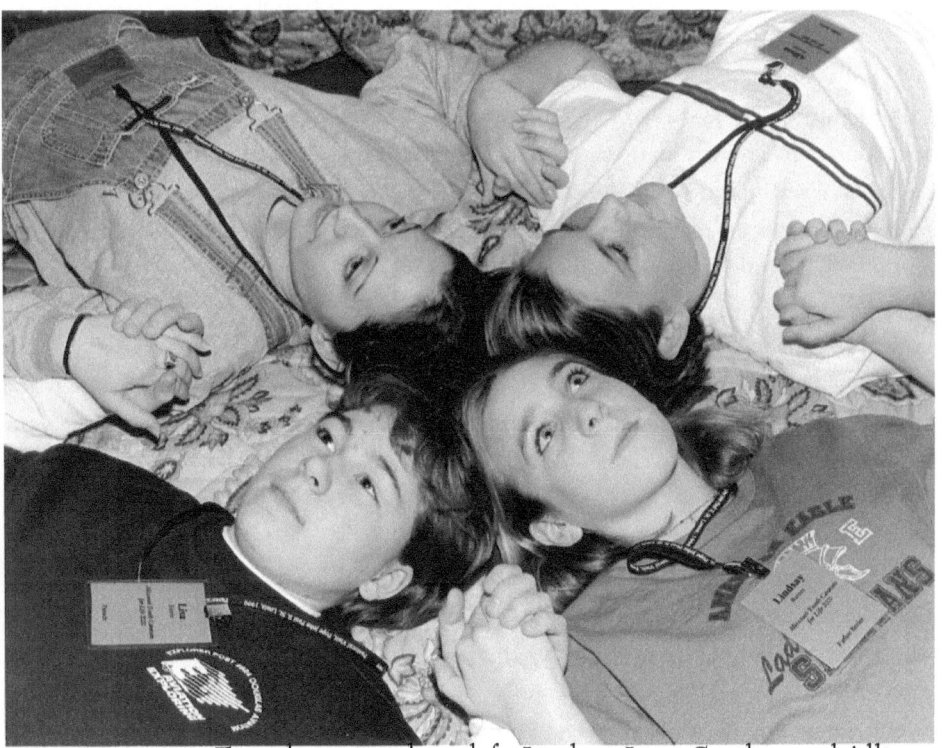

From bottom right to left: Lindsay, Lisa, Carolyn, and Allison

Catherine 17

My parents are Italian, both of them and I was adopted from South Korea, Seoul. I came to the United States... actually, I came to Rochester when I was two and a half months. Then we move from there to Syracuse. I was the first child and oldest to come. After my dad got his graduate's degree in Rochester, we moved to Syracuse.

When did you first realize you were adopted?
I think I always knew. Like I can remember, I asked my parents that question and they said you could identify that you were different. You look at magazines and pick out Asians and say that looks like me. So I think I've always known and my mom works for *Love the Children*, an adoption agency for children. I would go with her, go to the airport and see what would happen, see the families come.

How do feel about being adopted?
There's stages. When I was young, I though it was really cool. Like maybe when I was first and second grade. Then later the influence of others came in, like your teenage, adolescent years.

How has your teenage years affected you?
I kept it more quite. If someone would ask, I would keep it to one-word answers. I wouldn't like to be different. Like my skin tans very easily, so in the summer I would get really tan. So I would try to prevent that. I try to be like everyone else.

When you say, "you would try to be like everyone else," what do you mean? Like talk like them or act like them?
I live in a very suburban town, very secluded, small and the majority of the students there are white Americans, small population of Asians. Very, very small population of Asians. In my grade, there's about twelve. Majority of them are Koreans. They come from Asian homes.

Do you talk to them about your culture?
Yeah, like my friend's mom would cook me food. I would hear their accent and that's really hard to understand.

Do you go to your friend's house often to get to know about your culture?
Not really. I've only been there a couple of times and just have friendly conversations and that's it.

How are your adopted parents towards you? Do they treat you well?
O yeah, very well. *They provided everything for me.* The best education. The best high school in the United States. They don't have any restrictions of what I can do. If I want to try a new sport, they would be very encouraging. If I don't feel well they will be sympathetic and they will be there. My mom doesn't work. She actually just finished her degree in nursing. My dad is a periodontist, which is your gum. So they're always around.

So do they have their own children?
Yes they do.

How many?
Two. We are all two years apart.

Do you all get along?
Yeah.

How do you feel now when you tell people that you are adopted? Do you feel fine and you don't mind telling people that you are adopted anymore?
I think I kinda grown out of that stage. Seeing that people live with certain things as I do and its not a big deal to them. You just kind of accept it and you mature when you grow and it's not a big issue anymore.

How old are you?
I will be 18 in March.

Have you ever wonder what are your birth parents are like? Have you try to find out where they are?
With these adoption, we are given record of their age and their names and all their background information.
I was offered a trip to Korea for my graduation present for next year, by my parents. She did offer we could do a search and find if I would like to. When she did go to

Young Sisters

Korea, when I was in fourth grade, she had to bring some children over on the plane. She did search and find on the lady who brought me on the plane. Who would take me to the United States and met her and showed her pictures. It was neat and fun.

So are you going to Korea for your graduation?
I don't know I have a year to think about it.

Have you ever found out why she....
In my records, both of them were in their twenties and very poor. So it was just the best decision. They were unmarried.

So do you think it was a good thing that they gave you up for adoption?
O yeah, I think it's a better decision.

Do you go anywhere to learn about your own culture and who you are being a Korean?
There is a camp in Rochester, for one week in August every year. I've been going there for nine years. And there are classes, you'll be divided into your age group. The counselors there are Koreans who brought up in a Korean home who knows the language and the culture in the back of their hand. We have culture class, language class, arts, and crafts, cooking, dance, newspaper.

How has those classes in Rochester help you to familiarize with yourself?
Just so I know where I come from. That I'm not the only adopted Korean, cause they are tons of kids there of all ages who has similar problems, questions, and interests. It's kind of reassuring.

Do you have anything to add?
It's probably the best decision. That could have happen.

Do you think you would adopt too when you grow older from this experience you have?
Maybe, probably.

Family

My Family

What can I say about my family. Well, I hate my brother and my sister. My mother, I love her, I hate her. My father, I love him, I hate him. This is how I feel almost every single time I get angry at them. I hate my brother and sister and wish I was the only child in my family. Sometimes I argue with my parents and get angry at them and wish I wasn't born. I sometimes see my parents argue and hear them yelling and I hate when this happens. So far I said the bad side of my family. But they are not always like this. Mainly they are alway happy. My brother playing with his action figures while my sister watching T.v or being a big suck up like allways. And my parents watching T.v. and talking to each other. But sometimes I am grateful I have great parents. I sometimes see in t.v shows like the maury show saying about bad teens and showing them how they treat there mother. They say bad thing to them. And I realize that this is rediculous. I mean, sure I do this sometimes

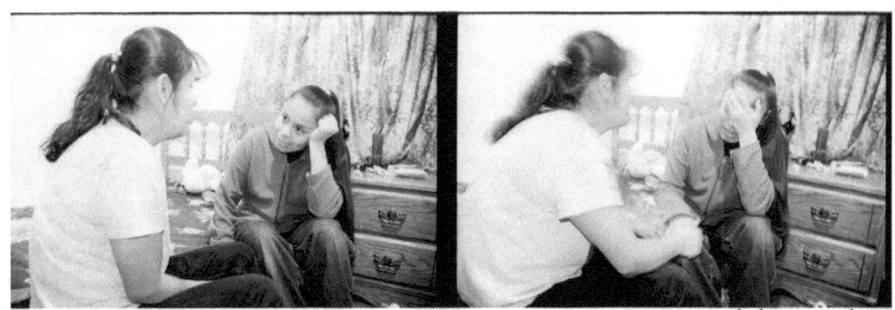

Jessica with her mother

to my mother and realize how mean I was.
I mean, when I had hard times in school
and need someone to talk to, my mom
was alway there. When I had problems
with my friend like for example I onces
remember that my best friend chose
between two girls to
be her friend over me. I felt hurt. My
mother was there. When I needed
someone to talk to my dad was there.
He was there to comfert me.

I didn't realize that I am lucky
to have a family like this. I
had friend that wish they had
a brother or a sister because they are
all alone and wish they had some
one to at least to beat them up.
Also I had someone show me
how lucky I was having parents
that at least talk to you and plays
with you, video games or at least
spending time with you. she had

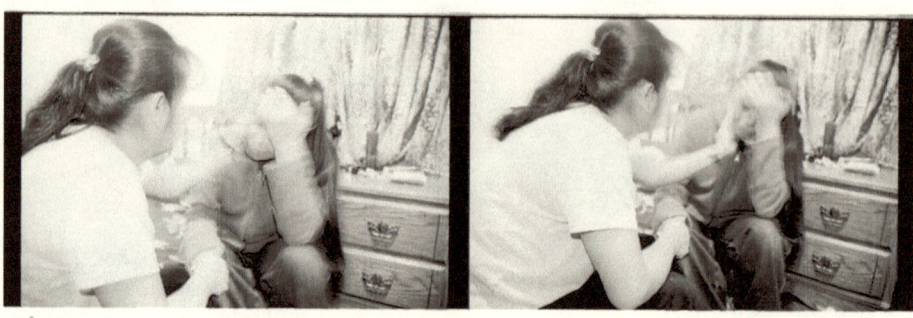

every thing. I was living the good time. I
mean she had things I wish I had
but couldn't because my parents wouldn't
buy it for me and I would usually
get mad. But the one thing I have
that she doesn't have is time or
communication with her parents.
She has a step mom and said
she doesn't get along with her.
The only thing she would
want is having at least one
minute with her parents and having
wishes she
communication with her parents.
After she told me I guess I saw
things in a different way. I realized that
I am Lucky having a brother and
a sister at least to beat them
up om playing wrestling with my
brother and having loving
parents. I know I can count on
and parents that care about.

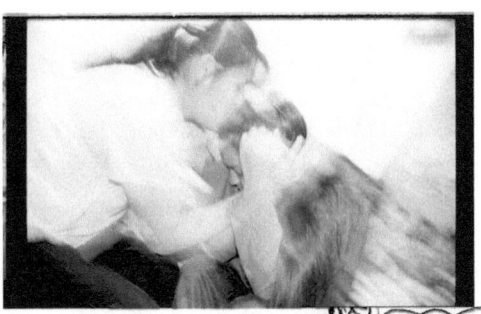

me. i may not ~~have a~~ ~~good~~ ~~live~~ ~~poor~~ have every thing I want or having a great life like you know a rich life But I have a ~~too~~ wealthy life. ~~and with a life that~~ a great family. that I am thankful for.

What I would like to say is that be grateful with what you have. and don't take things for grandted. You may say we don't need our porent ~~and~~ or I hate them But at least you have someone that loves you and that will always be there for you. Many people wish they had someone ~~that aren't~~ ~~telling~~ like that, You know.

Young Sisters

Anonymous
Age: 17

This summer, for the first time, I had to move away from my family. It was because of a summer program I needed to attend for college. I felt sad and really nervous and scared because now I would be on my own and would not be able to depend on my family for every little thing. The person I would miss the most is my mother. We always had a close relationship and I saw her every day since I was a baby. She was sad to see me go and even cried a little the day I left. When I got to the college, people greeted me very nicely, so I felt better. My roommate is cool. I am used to everything now and have met new people that are really nice. I like the atmosphere. I guess sometimes you just gotta let go and do what you gotta do. I myself hate change, but once you get used to it, everything falls into place.

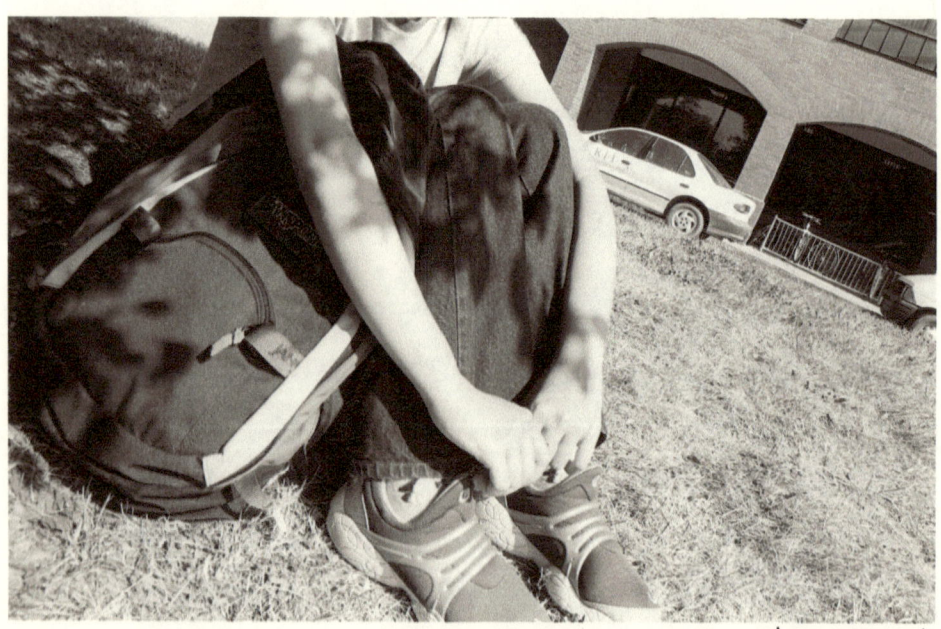

Anonymous 1

In Jamaica now-a-days alot of people are leaving, because of crime, jobs, or school. And sometimes its hard, because when you get close to some one they have to leave. ...And some of my friends in my class will be leaving in a couple of months, like Tiffany Chin. She's chines-Jamaican and she's going away to Miami for school.

But my hardest loss was my cousin/best friend, Annalise.

Anna is mixed, 13 years old, smart, pretty, fun, has 3 brothers, and says her hobbies are playing basketball, eating, sleeping, and reading! She moved because her father was looking for a job in Christian Film Production, first they moved to Virginia then to Oregon. The last time I saw her was 2 summers ago (year 2000) And I miss her sooo... much! She left 3½ years ago (year 1998.) when she was 9. But we do keep intouch by emailing and messenger, But I do have other close friends ... Appreciate them! Dont take them for granted! You wont realise how much they meant to you until they're gone!

— Jessica
13 yrs. old
Jamaica,
West Indies.

"I just tell them to cherish the time they have. Your mother, your father, anybody. They might get on your nerves, you might get mad at them, but life is too short. We're not going to be here forever. Just spend as much time as you can with them. Just love them and show them how much you love them, because they are not always going to be there for you. You're really gonna regret it when they are gone."

Chantel 16

Losing Someone

Chantel 16

Tell me about your grandmother. Tell me about the past you had with her and how she's special to you.
Her name was Clara and she died of breast cancer on April 13. I moved here from Arkansas when I was seven-years-old. I came to live with her and *she dedicated her life to me.* She taught me almost everything that I knew. When I was little we went to church together, she always dress me in my little dresses and my little hat. She took me shopping. I was the only grandchild, I was the first-born of my mother. I spend so much time with her and I thought she would never... I didn't know about her illness until two years ago. I thought she would never leave me, I thought she would be here forever. She always told me to go to school, go to college. She wanted me to be successful. She was so smart, it was like she knew everything. She had no enemies. She was very unselfish. She always thought of other people's well being before her own. And that *made her so special.* It really did.

Are you afraid that you might get breast cancer too since its hereditary?
I don't really think about it as much, I know it's hereditary. I'm not afraid. I know she went through it and she...she...she was so strong. And I know if I were to die from it I would be as strong as she was. And I just have to live with it, because everybody has to die sometime. I'm not really scared. I try not to think about it. I try to live life to the fullest and that's it.

What were your feelings when you found out that she had breast cancer and she was going to leave you?
When I found out, I was really depressed. I wasn't crying. I didn't think she was going to die. I thought she will have breast cancer, she'll get treatment for it and it will be all right. She wasn't supposed to get sick. And when she got sick a couple of months before she passed away, I was really scared. I was there everyday at her house after school. I would cook for her. I would be right by her bedside. I would tell her about school and everything and then she really...it got worst. And one night when I was sitting by my bed my mother came in and told me and I started crying because... I knew she was going to go, because of how sick she was, but I didn't think it would be that soon. I wasn't really ready and it really hurt me.

How much do you miss her now? Like do you think about her all the time?
I think about her everyday. I miss her a lot. I think about all the stuff that we use to do together. Sometimes she would tell me to come over there, but I would be busy doing something. So now I regret not going. I'll be like, "O, I should have went." That's some of the time that I missed out on her. I wish she was here today. If I can get her back I would want to be with her everyday, I wouldn't even go home. I'll just live with her forever. I wish I can turn back in time, but I can't.

What is your message for people who have love ones right now, and is taking advantage of them, and not spending valuable time with them?
I just tell them to cherish the time they have. Your mother, your father, anybody. They might get on your nerves, you might get mad at them, but life is too short. We're not going to be here forever. Just spend as much time as you can with them. Just love them and show them how much you love them, because they are not always going to be there for you. You're really gonna regret it when they are gone.

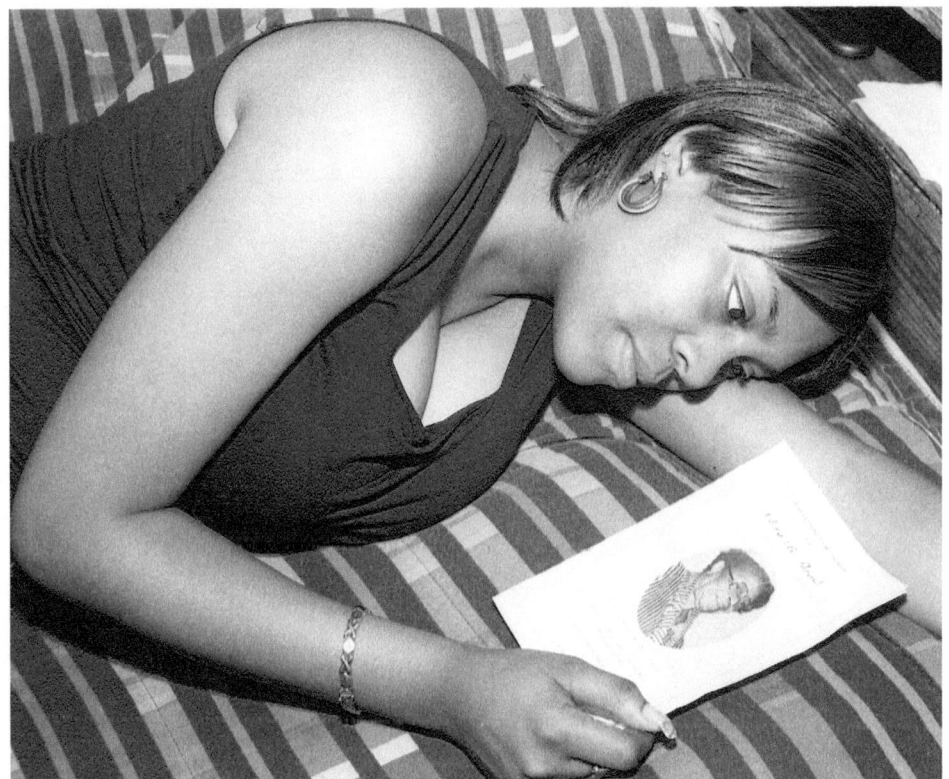

Chantel

Young Sisters

Nyasha 18

I was 14 yrs old when I was told that my sister had past. It was totally unexpected to me, eventhough I knew that she was sick, I felt shock It took 2 yrs to actually understand it, to believe her death.

My sister and I were very good friends. We would sing and dance together. She alway knew what to say when I was sad. She was special to me because we alway had this bond that was unexplainable. Growing up with 5 other sisters was hard but she had charisma. She taught me how to sing and dance.

I don't have any regret when it comes to not appreciating her, but I do because she's not here to sing our song. It went "your my brother, you're my sister so take me by the hand together we'll work it out." Oh how I miss her.

No she never gave me anything that now has meaning to me except our song. Yes I do feel my sister's presence around me protecting me and guiding me, whenever I get lost. I guess like my guarding Angel

Now that my sister is gone. I'm last, and that make me feel weak, because I don't know whether or not I can do it on my own, but like I said before I'm in hopes that her presence will guide me.

For anyone who have ever lost someone
close to them, it doesn't have to be a
family member, but just as close.
My advise to you is don't give up in your
faith, because they wouldn't want you to.
Don't give up on life just strive harder
to show them that everything they've
taught you didn't go in vain

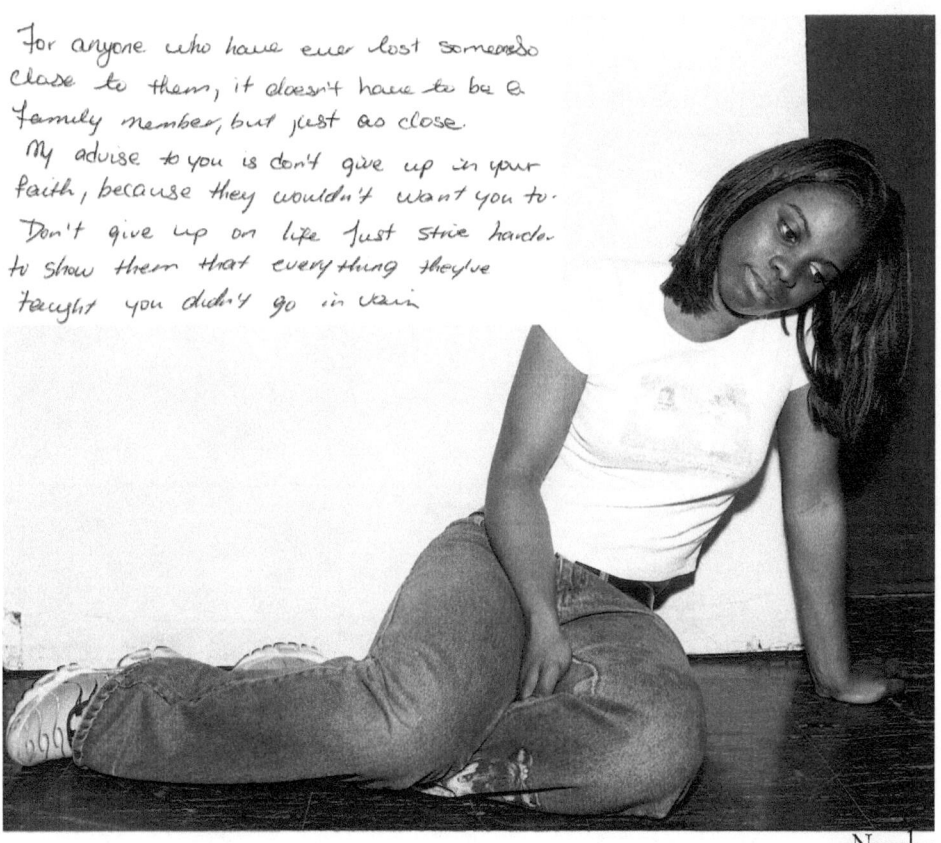

Nyasha

"Trust me these things are easier said than done.
After going through all of these things I am blessed that I am who I am."

Shonta 18

A Hard Knock Life

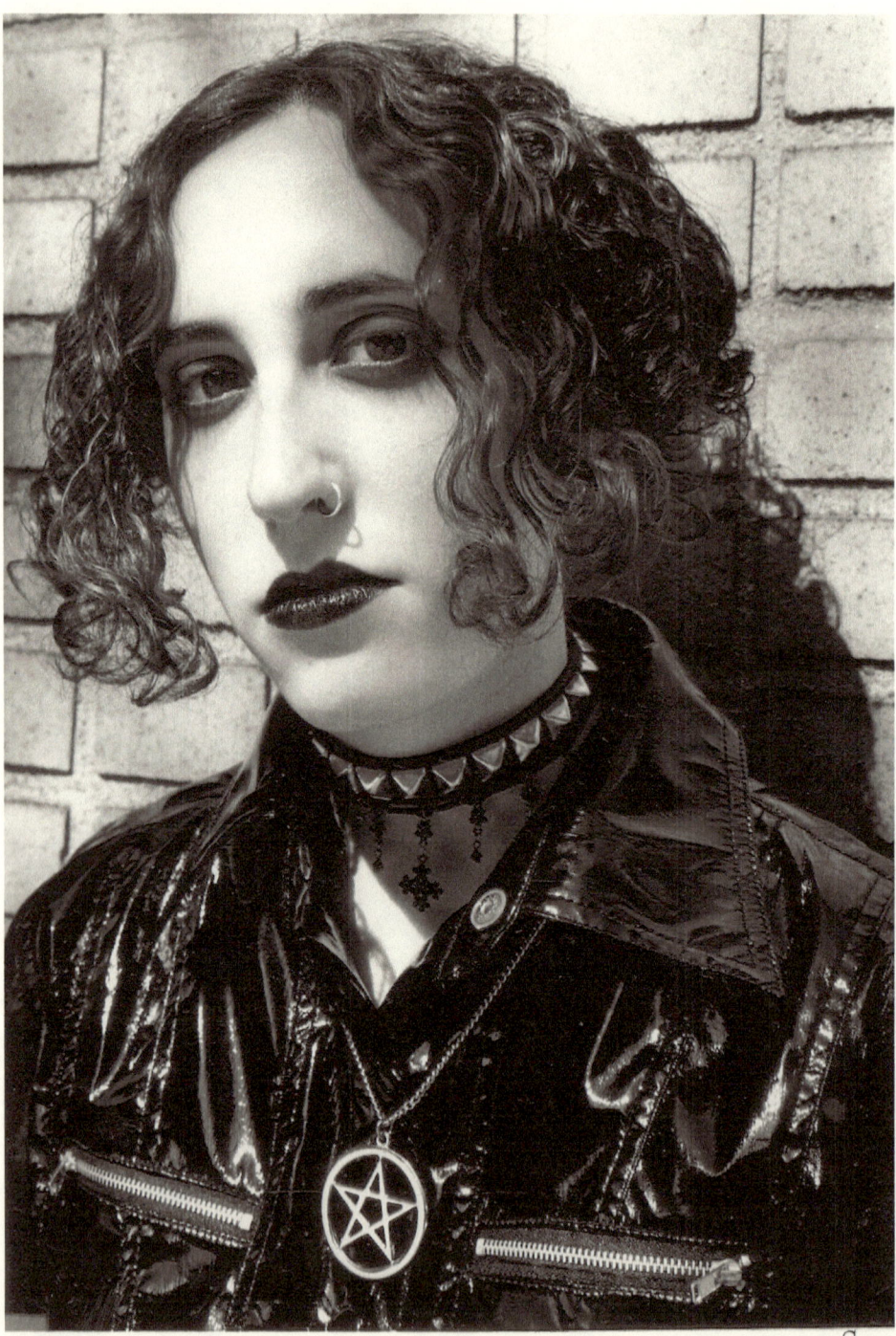

Sam

Sam

I remember the first time I smoked weed was in eight grade on May 9, it was my friend's birthday party. We were all hanging out outside and I heard this kid had weed, you know, and I always wanted to try it. Just to experience it. I tried it and I felt fine but the next day everyone was telling me that I was acting like a moron. Sooo, I guest that was my first experience with drugs. The first time I really didn't feel anything and I was like, "this sucks" I was expecting it to feel a little bit different. But after a while, I started to do it more and more. I started to get fucked up. And I was like "Wow, this is pretty cool." So I did like it.

Everything I tried was weed, acid, ecstasy,... coke, umm....hmm..... weed with other stuff, god knows what, umm, whippids, strooms, rush and that's basically it. I don't think I've tried anything else unless it was slipped to me.

Acid is LSD. You take it on a tab, a little square piece of paper. And what it does it's just like after about twenty minutes or so, you start feeling really weird and you see weird shit. The first few time I tripped, I really didn't see much except for sun trails. Then later on, like one day, I tried it on my junior high school reunion dance that was the first time I saw major visuals and you know I saw major trails. Everything was so colorful and weird. It was bugging me out. I was like "O shiiit" But it was pretty cool.

Sometimes you can have really good trips, nothing bothers you, you are just chilling, sitting there, watching everything happen and you're listening to music and everything just goes through you. It's a really cool experience, but other times you can really bug out. Like one time I had a really bad trip with my friends. I guess it was because of the neighborhood we were in. We were really scared. I got bugged out. And there are other times where my friends and I were listening to Jimmy Hendricks and it was the best trip I've ever had.

Well ecstasy, you can have it in pill forms or whatever. What is it is....it's...uhhhhh, how can I explain it. It contains different types of drugs. It contains coke, speed, heroin among other things. What it does, is you take it and it gives you eternal bliss. You feel really happy and you love everyone around you. I mean like the first time I did it, I was so gone, because I took coke right before that it was really fucked up. And the coke with ecstasy and including what I took before. I was gone. My friends and I felt like we were flying. I cannot explain that feeling. I mean like it was just amazing! You know. It was just a fun feeling.

Shrooms is a mushroom grown in different places like cow shit some place. I don't know where it is grown exactly. I only did that once this summer, because I stopped doing psycadelic stuff. Like acid, I stopped doing that, because every time I tripped I would had a fucked up one. And I would bugged out so I didn't want to do that anymore. But shrooms I wanted to try it for the experience. And I tried it and it was really amazing. I closed my eyes and I would see different colors, shapes and patterns and I felt like Buddha, I can't explain the feeling it was just fucking amazing. It is basically like acid but it is a lot more colorful. It's a different experience.

Coke is white powder, blah blah blah. With that I always said to myself I would never try that and I would never try heroin, which I haven't, thank god. I know people who have and that just bugs me out. But coke I don't know. Its cool, but I only did it a few times cause I never wanted to get into that cause I was paranoid about ODing (over dose) with a heart attack or something. The one time that I did try it was cool. Personally, I don't understand why people do it so much. All you do is get mad hyper and give you a good feeling, but it last like 20 minutes and that's it. Done. Dead. Done. Its cool while you do it but I never got into that. I just did it a few times last year and that was it.

Whippeds is like you know whipped cream. You shake it and it comes out with that gas. Its like when you inhale it, it makes you all numb and weird and like its fucking cool. Me and my friends used to do it, like having a few in a row. And you feel really fucked up, but like we didn't realized that, that shit can kill you and some kids have died from that, because it goes straight to your brain. And it stops air going in there or something stupid, but we did it anyway. I don't know, two years ago I was a lot more dumb.

Another thing that we used to do is this thing called Rush and what you do is you inhale it and you get this really good head rush and you feel all warm. Its pretty weird but I never really like to begin with it, because whenever I finish doing it I always get headaches. It was pretty shitty, but all my friends like it. So we used to buy that.

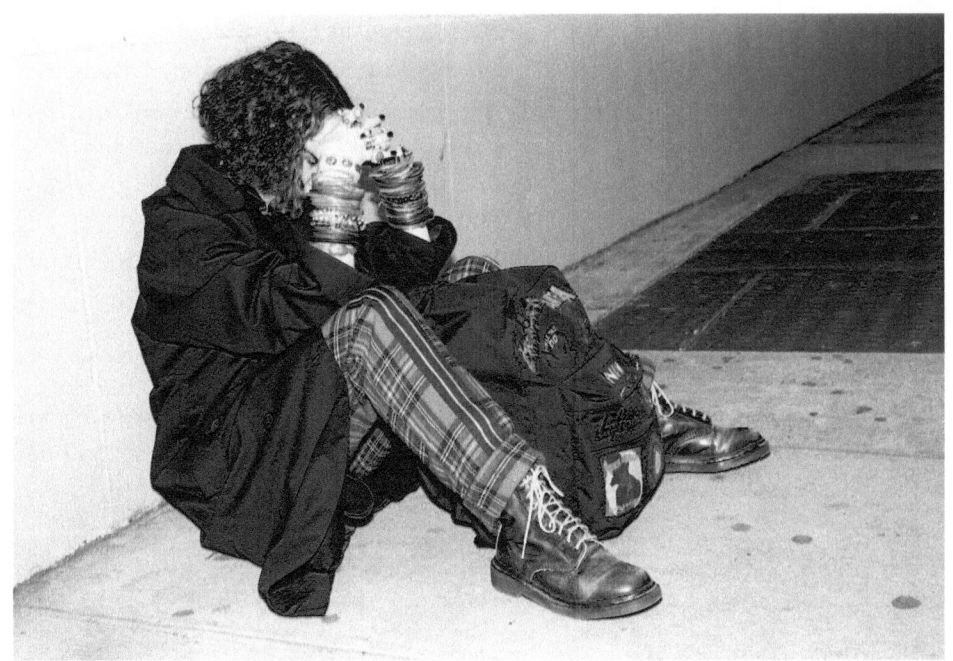

Two years ago, freshmen year, I used to spend like.... It really buggs me out on how much money I would spend every week. I spend $20 on whippeds, that's one box of 25 for $10. I used money for weed, spend money on tabs. And only last year, I started doing ecstasy. This year, I'm doing pretty good. I haven't really smoked. I smoked twice in the past four months.

My theory on liquor is personally I don't like drinking, because it reminds me of my father and he's like a dumb drunk. Yes, I drink sometimes, but its usually not beer, its like liquor that taste good, like winecoolers. I drink enough and get buzz. Although one time, I got really, really, really drunk and the was the stupidess...like I have never felt so embarrass. It was this summer and I was at *Jose's backyard, it was the last day before he was moving. I brought a six pack of beer all for myself, I drunk four out six of them then I had a Bud, then I take sips from everyone's beer, liquor, and whatever fuck they were drinking. I was so fucked up to the point that the room was spinning, I could not walk straight, I could not stand, I had to lean on my friends, lean on the wall to get to the yard, cause we were all the way up stairs and we have to get down stairs and out, cause we have to go to the yard. It was so fucked up. I was making such a fool out of myself. When you get drunk, drunk like that you just get really emotional and you let your feelings come out. Its kind of like being on E. All of a sudden, I started liking Jose. And my friends were like, "Sam, calm down." Cause my friends were pretty sober. And I was like, "No, no, no, I really love him." I started screaming, "I love him" and all that shit. I was making a fool out of myself.

At this point we were at the yard, I started puking. It was horrible and my friends left and I was sleeping all by myself. Jose came over to me and told me that I need to calm down. I was crying and I was saying, "I love you."

I was pretty fucked up the next day and wreck and sick. My mom asked me if I was drinking. I knew if she knew that I was drinking she would kick my ass. So I lied so I wouldn't get my ass kicked.

Every time I take a new drug, I have to know some of its history. I know basically what happens but like when I take it I expect a certain thing but it turns out a different way. When I tried E, I had no idea what the hell was gonna happen. My friends were telling me that it was the best thing in the world, but I was like how do I know. So when I took it, I was waiting for something to happen. And all of a sudden out of no where. Bam. I was feeling like all weird and crazy.

We used to be not paranoid at all about getting caught. Like we would smoke up joint in the middle of the street. We just didn't give a shit, we had pipes, we just walk around smoking. Now, we are always paranoid. We are like, "O shit, are there any cops here? Did cops bust anyone lately?" We would ask questions like that. Sometimes I'll be paranoid about cops. Being paranoid that it would be fucking me up. Like something bad happening. The only thing that I was really, really, really concern with was when I did coke. I was always paranoid that someone was going to OD me. Like New Year's eve last year, all I did was watch my friends do a 57 or 8 ball or how ever much they had. They just kept on sniffing and sniffing, I was waiting for someone nose's to start bleeding, going into convulsions, that would just fuck me up.

Now I am pretty much sober. I like being sober. Whenever I used to get stone or on anything, I would always act a certain way, I would act weird towards people and I would always get depressed and down and distant. Like I would be so in love with someone and it just push me down even more with the drugs. All my emotions are mixed with the drugs, it would make it ten times worst than it would be and I don't need that shit. When I started being sober, I started realizing that I don't need that. I like being sober. Yeah I still get fucked up once in a while with friends when I hang out because I don't hang out half as much as I used to. But when I do get fucked up, I do know my limits. I know if I start feeling that feeling I don't like, I stop. And no one pressures me to do anything. Its just like ok and their cool and they continue to get fucked up.

If people want to try drugs I would warn them about the circumstances. At first its yes its fun and games. Its fun, you like to do it, you do it a lot. I would just say to watch out and know your limits. You shouldn't go to a certain point that you are going to OD or you are going to hurt yourself in the end. Cause that is what I think me and my friends did. We didn't think about this shit at all. We just kept on doing and doing it and not having second thoughts about it. In the end, we are all totally fucked up. And that is just how it is, because we didn't stop when we should have. We just kept on going and going like an energizer fucking bunny.

I never went to rehab. I just said, I don't feel like doing this anymore and I stop. One of my friend just stopped after a bad tripped, but he still see shit. He has to go to a specialist. The one person that I'm really worry about now is Jose. He just keeps on doing it more and more. He does coke now. I just found out from my friends, which I'm not even suppose to know, because Jose thought if I knew I wouldn't be friends with him anymore. That he was doing heroin every day of the whole summer. I didn't know this and it really upset me that he couldn't even tell me, that he was afraid that I wouldn't be friends with him anymore. I mean for him to even think that, it was wrong. I am just really worried about him, because I seriously would not be surprise if I got called up one day that he fucking OD for something.

Shakeya 17

I'm Shakeya. I'm seventeen-years-old. I've been living in a group home since September 21, 1999.

How did you get in there?
Well, that story will open up to a whole lot of questions. But ummm, I first got place in a group home, because of my abusive mother and I had told a lady at my job, my boss and she reported it, her and another lady. And come to find out the lady she report it to we had already knew her from years ago me and my sister and family. She was a supervisor at the Salvation Army Group Homes. Two of them, Crony House and Burnside. She asked my mother if we could spend the night with her and that one night turned into a whole week. And then ECS (Emergency Child Services) came in the middle of the night and told us that, "If we didn't go home and stop lying about my mother, then Mr. *Frank will be arrested and we're gonna be charge as runaways which means we are going to get a PINS (Persons In Need of Supervision) warrant. And when you get a PINS warrant that's like an offense. You can be sentence to anything. You could be locked up. You could be send to a detention center. So we went home the next day.

So you were at the group home for a whole week?
No, I stay with this lady for a whole week. Once we went home, the ACS (Association of Child Services) worker told my mother that we were liars, that he felt bad for us that we have to lie to get freedom. When we found out about this we have reported to Ms. *Cost, but there was not much she could do about it because my mother was threaten to have her job taken by mentioning things that happened in her pass. The ACS worker, Mr. *Lee, I could never forget his name because I told him, "If you sent me home, then I am going to get my ass beat up all over again." So he didn't believe me and he send me back home and said, "If your mother hit you again then I'll move you." So we were there, nothing ever changed. She kept calling us this, kept calling us that. So I figure the only way I was going to get out of here is if I get her to hit me. So I didn't hit her. I just kinda started the conflict very quick. I was talking to my friend on the phone when I knew I wasn't suppose to be on the phone. Just so I can proof to them that she does stuff like this and nobody believe me. So we ended up fighting. And I had rings on all my fingers and she bite on one of my rings into my finger and I still have the bruise and she has sprained

this hand. So the next day, ACS came to pick me up at my job. And from there I went to Light Street, and from Light Street I went to the Teen Center, and from Teen Center I went to 34th and Clarity.

How has your life changed since you moved out of your home and lived in a group home?
Well, its kind of up and down. When I first moved into the group home. I was still the same innocent Shakeya I was when I lived at home. There was a lot things I had to learn. Like I have to learn how to take care of myself. I had to learn how to survive. I had to learn how to become an independent child at the age of fifteen and it was hard, because no one should be forced to be an adult at fifteen. You don't really start becoming an adult until you are in your twenties. I had to survive and become an adult for Shakeya. It has made me a good and bad person, because with becoming an adult there are lessons you have to learn. Stuff that I wasn't ready to experience, I had to experience and learn for myself.

Can you give me some examples? Or is it too personal?
No its not too personal. Well, as far as.......hmmm. Let me see. As far as....umm, money, you know. Before I moved into the group home, I sold drugs. But not on a regular bases. But when I first moved into a group, I realized, if you don't have any money then you can't get nothing. So then I started back selling drugs and .....I feel, I felt...now that I think about it, I feel kind of sorry for myself. Because what was I doing selling drugs at fifteen. Why wasn't my mother... didn't take care of me and buy me the things that I need. You know support me the way she was suppose to. So I had to support Shakeya. You know. I had to learn and figure out the streets, I had to survive. I had to make money so I can buy this and buy that for Shakeya you know and its kind of sad, because I see it happen all the time. And I was a fifteen-year-old drug dealer, selling drugs to lawyers and doctors and businessmen, cause that's where the money was at. I even sold drugs to like little kids, like twelve-year-olds.

Did you feel bad when you sell drugs to the little kids?
I felt horrible. I taught a ten-year-old boy how to sniff coke. Because he came to me to buy drugs and he didn't even know how to take the drugs. You know. So what are you doing at ten or eleven-years-old trying to do something that you don't even know how to do. You know. And I feel like I have ruin his life. For the rest of his life, he could become a coke addict and it would be my fault. Because I taught him how to do it or because I needed that money.

Young Sisters

You are not selling drugs anymore right?
No.

Well, what are you doing now to get money?
Well, I was working. I was a certified lifeguard. I've been working as a lifeguard since I was sixteen, but I just quit recently.

You mentioned you had a sister. Was she in the group home with you?
No, I have two sisters. My mother would switch sides. Like one minute, she would beat the hell out of me and the next minute she would beat the hell out of *Sasha and back and forth and back and forth like that. She put us both out at the same time. I went to a group home and Sasha went to a covenant house and its a shelter. It is one of the worst shelter I've ever seen. And I wouldn't wish this on my worst enemy. Because my place was voluntary, I'm in what you called it a voluntary placement. Where you go to ACS and tell them, "Look, I'm being abused, take me away from this." But when I enter the group home I thought it was going to be a lot different than living at home. Its not too different. The only thing is, I'm not getting abused. But its not that much of a difference. The females there, they still disrespect you. They deny you almost everything they can.

Are you talking about the employers there?
I'm talking about the caseworkers. And when you go complain to the right type of people, they don't listen to you. But when you take matters into your own hands, they think you're crazy. They want to give you all type of medications to tame you like you are a beast or something. When all you trying to do is to show somebody that this person is not treating me right. And they ignore you. They look at you like a walking dollar sign, like if they lose your business then that is the money they are losing out on. As long as you are alive, they don't care what happens to you.

So at the group home you are not happy, but you are not being abuse and its just a place that you live.
Exactly. The only reason why any girl or guy in a group home would never want to go home is the freedom. I don't want to say I left home to be free, to be able to go out whenever I want to and stay out as long as I want. That comes along with it but that's not the reason why I would report my mother to ACS. But that's the reason why I don't want to go back home. But one thing, I know what I would go through when I go back

home. I know that I'm never going to be respected. I'm never going to be look at as a person, as a human being. All my mother is going to see is a maid, a punching bag, and someone who you would take your anger out on. I don't have to be at a group home. And I could defend myself at a group home. When I live at home, I couldn't defend myself, cause I couldn't do that to my mother. I'm raised by how people were raised in South Carolina, you respected your parents. No matter what they do, its tough love, and that is how she said it to me. But I don't believe that now, I think its just bullshit. Now that I am in a situation that I can defend me and take care of Shakeya and I can be independent. I wouldn't want to change that for the world.

How has the group home change you in terms of making you more aware there's other people like you?

It did put through a lot of things, because I didn't know what a group home was until I moved there. I thought that I had problems and my life was the worst, I meet people everyday, girls that pass through the group home who...I thought I had it bad, they had it horrible you know. At least I know who my mother is. There're girls who don't know who their parents are. There's girls who know who there mother was, because their mother was never ever there for them. You know, they experience sexual abuse living at home with their parents. And I can say that I'm kind of glad that I have never experience sexual abuse. There's girls who are Special ED, who are born practically retarded, because their parents did drugs with them. My mother was never a drug user.

For the record, I don't want to say that my mother was the worst parent in the world, because she always took care of her three daughters. Wherever she was, her three girls was with her. But moving into the group home, some girls don't' even call their mother, their mother. I recognize my mother is my mother, but there's girls who say, "Who is she? She's nobody. She never took care of me." So I feel bad. A lot of girls had it bad. The group home has definitely changed me. It hurt me. The group home has hurted me. This morning I made up my mind that I don't want to live at a group home anymore. I don't know what I'm going to do. They are kicking everybody out soon. And turning it into a harder place home for mentally disturb girls and girls with a lot of problems and I am not one of those girls. I have one friend in the group home and that's my roommate and she's gonna have to leave soon too. We all gonna have to leave. We are living in a construction site right now. The house is being rebuilt, all over our heads with us right there.

When I lived at home. There was not rats in my house, there was no mice, there was no stink girls. You know, nothing like that. I get sick of waking up in the morning and seeing girls who just don't give a shit about themselves. Who don't care how they look. Who don't care how they speak. You know, who just don't care. I can't stand to see that, I'm sick of seeing it. In September 21, it will make two years. I don't have to experience shit like this and I'm sick of it, I don't deserve it, I didn't ask for this. All I ask was that my mother to stop beating the shit out of me.

Where are you going now? Are you going to look for an apartment to live with your girlfriends?
I have not idea. I don't want to live with any girls. I'm sick of living with girls. I don't know what I'm going to do, but I know that I get discharge on September going into the Army and that's what I'm looking forward to. Everything else don't really matter. I guess I'll worry about it when it comes, but I'm not going to stress myself about it.

Do you have anything to add?
My advise would be to a lot of girls who are being abuse or a lot guys who are being abuse is that sometimes they don't recognize it. You have to recognize your abuse. Because for a long time, for fifteen years, I had no idea that I was being abuse. You have to know that you are being abuse and a lot of people don't realize it. But if it gets to a point where you feel like you don't want to live anymore. That you want to walk across the street and pray that a car would just hit you so you don't have to deal with this no more, then you know you are being abuse. And your life is not good and you need to take care of yourself and you need to survive. Its all about survival. And survival of the fittest, Darwin's theory is very true. You have to survive and this is a big ass world and people forget you like that, you know. So you have to make sure that you remember and you survive. Cause it's a hard knock life. A lot of girls don't realize it. I speak for girls, cause I am a girl. I can only speak from my point of view, but a lot girls are unaware and you have to make yourself aware. And you have to **respect** the world around you and don't burn your bridges. Because living in a group home has definitely made me an angry individual. Being abused and living around a mother who's always angry and violent, you know what I mean? It has made me an angry person. But you have to respect the people who try. Who try to help you. Don't think that the world is against you, because you can easily think the world is against you, because sometimes it is, but make your place in it you know. *Don't burn your bridges,* because you're going to need somebody some day. Whether it's a year from now or twenty years from now. There's going to be a person who you want to say, "Could you help me do this?" and always say "Thank you." Always let somebody know that you appreciate what they done for you, because the small things are always going to matter not all the big extra shit, you know.

Shontá

18

Daddy's Little Girl?

I remember a story someone once told me about a little girl and her father. She had always been daddy's little girl and would always be. daddys little girl. She had a special place in his heart for she was his youngest and the only child he had with his current wife. He had never been married before but he and his wife both had children before they married. This father spoiled his little girl to death; anything she asked for, he bought it. Even though he had two jobs and at one point three, he always found time to spend with his daughter. He was a great family man, he and his family went out Bike riding at least twice a month, and they even went out into grocery shopping together.

The little girl always drawn to her father for affection because her mother did not care much for hugging. Every night she gave her father a hug and kiss before she went to bed and her mother tucked her in. Life seemed good. The little girl had a next to perfect life with a wonderful family. She received good grades in school and had great friends. Anyone looking from the outside in would have seen a healthy lifestyle but there was something deeper that no one saw.

Her mother had to work during the day when summer began and the little girl stayed home with her father. Her father always found things to do together whether it was going out for lunch or just the two of them

going bike riding. The little girl always knew her
father loved her. ~~Because~~ He always touched her,
Even while they were watching television. Sometimes
he would let her sit on his lap when they watched
cartoons. Often he would rub her inner thighs and
tell her everything was okay, but remember don't
tell mommy, daddy loves you ~~As long as she could~~
~~remember this happened;~~ she thought daddy
~~does really love me he loves me more than he loves mommy.~~

As time went on, her father started to show
her more and more how much he *loved her.
~~As long as she could remember, her father showed how much he~~
Her father's intimate touch became the norm and
she thought nothing of it. Her father's ~~loved~~ expressive
behavior had gone on as long as she could remember.
One day he did something really special or so ~~she~~
thought. ~~For~~ Years he had ~~only~~ routinely rubbed her
body telling her that he was trying to relax her. On
this one particular day he put his finger in what her
mother called her private spot. The little girl jumped from
the pain and her daddy said, "It's okay if you
learn to love it the pain will go away." The only
problem was she never loved it but thought if she didn't
pretend, daddy would stop loving her.

~~When she was~~ The summer of her third grade
year her daddy showed her his ultimate sight of
love for her. He ~~gently~~ gently laid her on his bed and began to
relax her body, then did the thing with his finger that
she was suppose to love. When he felt that she was relaxed
he shoved his manhood into her now ~~tainted~~ spot and
began to unrighteously corrupt her body. As she
screams & pants in excruciating pain he continues to

show his love for her. For a minute he stops, and pulls out & puts vasoline on his ~~pulsating~~ erected object. Slowly ~~puts~~ eases it back in and continues only this time slower to calm the pain. When he has finished his business he ~~got~~ up and ~~goes~~ went to the bathroom. Now the daughter gets up and runs to her room as fast as possible. When she gets to her room she grabs a washcloth sneaks into her bathroom and locks the door. ~~While~~ As she is washing off her pulsating vagina tears stream down her face as she thinks, "I thought daddy loved me and would never hurt me." The little girl ~~The little girl~~ still acted normal when her mother was around, still gave her father good night hugs so her mother wouldn't think anything was wrong.

In the middle of her third grade year, one of the school guidance counselors came into the class to give a ~~speech~~ on good touch/bad touch. As the 8 year old listened to the ~~bad~~ examples of touches like on her private spot and rubbing her body causing her to feel uncomfortable not relaxed, she thought "why me. My father sexually abused me"

After the lecture the little girl sat her best friend down and explained to her what happened with her father and what happened that summer. Her best friend urged her to tell the guidance counselor. That night when the girl got home she told her mother instead of the guidance counselor. Her mother did not seemed surprised. Actually her mother ~~registered~~ said she knew that it was going to happen. She was in complete denial that her husband would do it to his own flesh-blood.

Soon she found out that those bad touches were called sexual abuse.

After after telling her mother about what happened she called over her niece and many family secrets began to surface. Little did the girl know her father had touched many others in the family. The girl was told that her father abused his other daughters, two of his nieces, two of his sisters, and my mother's other daughter. The girl was astonished but now she didn't feel alone. The only catch was now the little girl had to tell her father about what she felt was sexual abuse. With the most terrified look in her eyes. scared out of her mind she watches her father walk into the front door. He sees his daughter, his wife, and his niece sitting in the living room with the weirdest look, nothing he'd seen before.

He comes in and says, "whats going on," in a humorous tone. The mother tells him to sit down and listen; at this point he locks eyes with his daughter, his pride and joy and she turns away. Her mother tells her to go ahead, and they are there. As the little girl begins to tell him what happened in school w/ the counselor and the things that happened between the two of them his face turned sour. The little girl got frightened and talked softer and softer until she was finished. Her father said she was lying and maybe she had confused with someone else, maybe one of her uncles or that she made it up because one of her aunts told her to. After this speech he storms out the door and speeds away. The little girl falls in her mother's arms and cries herself tired.

The next day at school the little girl takes her best-friend to the guidance counselor's office and tells her what happened the night before at home. She goes back to class and a couple hours later the guidance counselor comes to her classroom and takes her back to her office. As she walks into the door she sees a woman & two men dressed very business like. They introduced themselves as Child Protector from Houston County. They took her to their offices and questioned her 4ors times recording it twice.

When her mother & her cousin came to pick her up they reminded her that she wasn't suppose to say anything to anyone. The Child Protector told her mother that she must move or her daughter would be taken away. They went home and packed a few of their things, her mom left a note for her husband telling him where they would be at a relative's.

They were away from him for about 1 year to a 9 months. During this year they moved out on their own, went to trial where the verdict was a hung jury, and moving back when charges were dropped. By this time it was the summer of her fifth grade year. Of course the little girl figured he had learned his lesson. He had lost his family and suffered consequences. During the 3½ months he stayed in the house he did not touch her inappropriately. One day, during school, the guidance counselor called her back down to her office. When the new 10 year old girl walked into the office she ran into the same business like people she saw 2 years earlier. They transfered her to a foster home where she stayed for 4 months; a nice couple. Her mother suggested that she move in w/ her aunt & uncle in Rochester, N.Y. since they were also doing foster care.

Now the little girl is no longer a little girl; she is young woman going into her freshman year of college at one of the top technical schools in the country. At the age of 18, this young woman has been through more things than the average teenager. Since the age of 10, when she arrived in New York, she has been hospitalized four times between the ages of 12 and 14. for depression. After having problems and disagreements at home her last hospital stay landed her in a group home. She was not in a group home because of illegal things, there were just problems at home.

At the age of 10½ she got into a program that gave aids to teenagers all expenses paid. This young woman sounds like an orphan but that was not the case. Her aunt/uncle were still there whenever she needed them. She still keeps in contact w/ her mother and speaks to her father after years of anguish. She has not seen him since she was 10 but she does speak to him on the phone. She sees her mother at least every two years. Most of the time she goes back to Georgia but her mother did attend her graduation.

Life is not perfect but she deals. She has problems range from family to boy trouble. After being abused as a child and overweight most of her life she has developed low self-confidence & esteem. After losing her virginity at 14 voluntarily she often mistaked sex for love. The older she got the better her confidence & esteem got, she is beginning to love herself inside & out. In spite of all the things she has gone through, she managed to do very well in school. She attended Our Lady of Mercy

7

High From 9, 9-12 grades. An all girl, Catholic, challenging school did not discourage her, school was her escape from her life that was far from normal. Often envying the girls she went to school with, who lived w/ both parents and lived very wealthy lifestyles, but they treated her like gold. She contributed a lot to this school. She did many extra-curricular activities ranging from step-team to Musicals to youth a gov't to school newspaper. Doing those things kept her mind off of her screwed life.

I am proud to say that she has grown up to be an intelligent young woman. Now learning who to trust as friends and keeping those who are she is doing pretty well. For you girls who have experienced some type of abuse whether sexual, emotional, or physical keep your head up. Don't let anyone put you down. Know what you are capable of and strive to achieve the best. Times aren't always going to be easy or clear but keep going. Set goals for yourself and don't worry about what other people think. That is the most important thing be yourself & trust in God. When someone tells you can't do something, or doubts you that's your life feel to achieve it.

Trust me these things are easier said than done. After going through all of these things I am blessed that I am who I am. The little girl in the story is me a my father sexually abused me. I have had a lot of support in my life and I thank God I am still alive. I love my father I will always be daddy's little girl
—Shonta, 18, N.Y.

Kimberly

Finding a Family

"It was my haven. It was the only place where I could go and feel like I could be myself. I didn't have to pretend, or put on a show for anyone, because the only person that mattered there was *Sarah. I needed that bench. I felt like I could go there and the rest of the world didn't matter." I paused, shocked that I had been able to put into words how I felt about something. I had never been able to talk about my feelings before then. They were always too overwhelming for me.

Then I heard *Kathy, my therapist, ask, "What in your life made you feel like you couldn't be like that all the time?" I looked up to see Kathy. She had a chubby face with huge glasses resting on her nose, and dressed like she was from the sixties. Kathy was always blunt and to the point. Even if I didn't want to talk about something, she would always find a way of making me deal with that was happening. I hated that in the process, but whenever I look back, I am grateful that I had a therapist who did that.

I pondered her question, and a tear rolled down my cheek and stopped at my chin. It was as though it was stuck and couldn't decide if it wanted to fall down and land God knows where, or if it could bear to part with me. It didn't know if it was better to take a chance and drop, or if it should just play it safe and wait there until it dried up. I was like that tear. I wasn't sure if I should take a chance and let my emotions out or if I should just hold on to them until they dried up and went away on their own because I was too scared of them to let them loose. I wiped the tear away from my chin. I decided to let it all out. I didn't know then that letting out all of my problems would be like a giant sandbag. Before I started talking about everything, my sandbag had a tiny hole in it and the sand would come out granule by granule. After I started to let her in on my life secrets, that tiny hole turned into a gigantic rip out of which the sand poured. I was about to get all of my problems out, so the burden wasn't on my shoulders anymore. I took a deep, shaky breath, and began:

The first thing that I can remember happening to me was my eldest brother *Eric molesting me when I was three years old. My parents would go out every Tuesday and Thursday night so they could, ironically, go to parenting seminars. Eric was left in charge of my other older brother *Fred, and I. Eric would send Fred to his room for some reason or another, and he would take me into the living room and do what he did. On one particular night, my parents' car broke down, and they came back early. They walked in to see me pulling up my panties and crying. They sent me to my room. I heard my parents talking to my brother in the kitchen and saying that what he was doing was illegal. Then my mom went into her room and read, and my dad went in the living room to fall asleep watching 'the game' on television. Reading, sleeping, watching sports were all favorite escapes for my parents. Whenever they refused to deal with something in their lives, that was what they turned to. My brother was never punished, and I was never consoled.

Looking back on it now, it all seems so weird to me. It wasn't strange back then. It was simply the way life was, or what I thought it was. I didn't know that what was happening to me was wrong, or that it wasn't happening to other people all over the world. I knew that it didn't feel right, but I just tried to ignore that feeling. I felt a shame for what was happening because my parents didn't do anything to protect me. They acted as though nothing was wrong.

Not long after this, my other brother Fred, was diagnosed as clinically depressed with episodes of paranoid schizophrenia. He was going through an extremely tough time, and would take all of his anger and frustration out on me. He would yell, threaten, hit, cut, and beat me up. My parents saw what he was doing to me. They chose to ignore the problem again. I remember running to my mom's room crying and wanting to tell her about a nightmare I had, or about my brother giving me a bruised and bloody face. I always had to wait until she turned the page in the book she was reading because she got mad at me when I interrupted her in the middle of a sentence, or paragraph. It was so painful for me to have to wait to tell her that I was hurting. I just stopped going in to talk to my mom. I didn't know what to do. I reached the point where I was scared to death whenever I was at home. I would lock myself in my room and pray while tears streaked down my face all day long. I can still hear myself. "Dear God, please let me not do anything to upset my brothers. Dear God, please let me..."

All of this affected me greatly. I became very depressed and passive. I felt as though I was at fault, and that I deserved to die. That's why I started to cut myself with razorblades. I honestly felt as though I was an awful person and that I deserved to be hurt. I would sit in my room on the brown carpet, roll up my sleeves and start to slash my arms. The carpet was the same color of the scabs and scars on my arms and reminded me of the once crimson trickle of blood running down my skin. It was soothing to see the blood come out of me. It was a reassurance that I was still alive. It made me feel real again. My emotional pain was so great that I didn't know how to deal with it. Cutting was my way of dealing with pain. It was almost cleansing, and I felt so much better during and after my cutting sessions. I was also always thinking about suicide, and different ways that I could end my suffering. I reached the point where I would do anything to get away from home.

While I was trying my hardest to stay as far away from home as I could get, I met my best friend *Sarah. Sarah was short, with cute feet. She had pale, milky colored skin with freckles all over it. Her long, straight, brown hair went to about the middle of her back. Sarah had olive green eyes framed in fake eyelashes that you could see the glue on (She didn't have real eyelashes, so she wore fake ones). She had pimples scattered about her face. Sarah was the first person that I was ever able to talk to about how I was feeling. Sarah made me feel as though I wasn't a freak, because she had a lot of the same thoughts that I did. She was depressed as well, so we were able to relate to each other. I belonged somewhere! We soon became inseparable. We reached a level in our friendship in which we could make each other forget our problems while we were together because we were having so much fun.

I began to feel like I was two separate people, leading two completely lives. Half of me was facing how it was when I was at home and how I felt inside almost all the time. The other half was how I acted in public with my friends; it was how I wished I could be all the time. I felt like I had bipolar disorder. I would go through stages of unbelievable happiness and giddiness, and then slip into a stage of severe depression. I felt that each time one of the stages would come or go the next one would be one hundred times worse than the last. I truly hated myself. I couldn't comprehend how my life could be the way it was. Sometimes the stages would engulf me for a few hours, or worse, a few days, or even weeks at a time.

My parents started to notice that I acted differently around my friends than I did at home, so they would listen in on my phone conversations. They heard me telling Sarah about how life was for me at home once, and smacked me silly. My father just stood back and watched with cold eyes as my mother grabbed my arm so hard it turned twenty shades of black, blue, and purple. She shook me while saying: "(Smack) If I hear you (Smack) tell anyone else (Smack) lies about my family again (Smack, smack), you won't have (Smack) a family (Smack) to complain (Smack) about anymore (Smack)."

Then my mother just let go and became hysterical. She started moaning about and crying to my father. I just cried. When I think about my phases that made my mother hate me even more, I think about the bench that Sarah and I would go sit on before school began just to talk. That is when I think that the stages I went through were quite apparent, because that was where I felt most comfortable with myself and my feelings. I didn't care what side of me came out; I could just let me surface.

Sarah and I would sit at the same spot in that dirty place. The bench was old and the wood on it was discolored. I could see litter all over the ground even though there was a trashcan across the hall, and groups of kids buzzed past us, blending into the background. There was a soda-pop machine in a cage right next to the bench. Graffiti covered the walls, ground, soda machine, and even our bench, but somehow there was a sense of beauty around us. Maybe it just looked so beautiful to me because I was at peace there.

One morning we would be talking, laughing, and telling jokes, and the next morning, a complete reversal. We sat in utter silence as I fought off tears because I hated my life, while Sarah sat there helpless, frustrated, and worried about me. I found it increasingly more difficult to hide how I was feeling. In my friendship with Sarah, I was desperately trying to create a family of my own. The family that I had was not a family to me. Sarah was there to love and support me when I needed it most. I can recall a recurring dream I had: I was walking around school following people around, but no one would talk to me, and it felt as though I was walking through water up to my waist. I couldn't keep up and my legs felt heavy. I think this dream was about how life was passing me by. I was stuck in this torturous existence.

Finally, I gained a firm grasp of my life, when I left my sorrows behind, and embarked on my now brighter future. Now I go to counseling once a week, and I like it a lot. I am learning so much about myself, and I really think that it has helped. I know that it wasn't my fault that I was neglected and abused while I grew up. It just happened. I can see that I am just as deserving of a person as everyone else, and can stand up for what I think and for what I believe in. I look people in the eyes and don't feel inferior. I've learned to love myself, and it is a wonderful feeling. I know that I am a strong person for having lived through the experiences that I have, and for trying to better myself. I would even go as far as to say that I am glad that everything happened to me that did, because if it didn't, I wouldn't be where I am today. It's like the old cliché: "What does not kill you, only makes you stronger,"

I lived in New York with my Aunt *Sue, and her family now. I feel like I am part of a family for the first time in my life. Just being around Sue, her husband *Cory, and their three boys: *Pete, *Jason, and *Ted, has shown me that having a loving family is possible. Sometimes, when I am in the kitchen helping to make dinner, one of Sue's boys will run in crying because he scraped his knee. Sue will stop what she is doing, even if it means burning the meal, put a bandage on the wound, and just hold him in her arms, rocking and kissing his tears until they go away. I can feel the love that emanates from them into every corner and cubbyhole of that house. At times it makes me sad because I never had that love growing up, but then I think about how lucky I am to have it now.

Being around a loving family had inspired me. I can't wait to start my own family some day; in fact, one of my main goals for the future is to be the best mother in the world for my kids. I am safe, happy, and loved where I am. I had never felt that way before in my entire life. I now have a place that I can finally call home, a house filled with one of the best families that God could ever give me.

Nichole 17

Do you do breast examination on yourself?
Yes, I do monthly checks.

What is the purpose of this examination?
The purpose of doing self breast examinations are to locate any lumps or anything that's irregular in your breast that can be harmful to your health.

Have you find anything?
Yes, I found a lump once.

When was this?
This was about two years ago.

Did you do anything about it?
When I first found the lump, I didn't say anything, I just kept it to myself. I kept it to myself for probably for about eight months, when I think about it now.

Why did you do that?
I didn't want to worry my family or myself. I convinced myself that it was nothing and that it would probably go away that it was just nothing.

So did you keep on doing the examinations on yourself and found the lump?
Um, like the next month after I had first found it, I kind of refrain from doing it. I didn't want to find it again and have to deal with it. So I did it the next month, but after a while of not doing it. I've decided that I still need to check even though I already knew it was there, because you can feel it, you know. So I decided to check and it was still there. But I still kept quite afterwards.

What made you finally to decide that, "Ok, I should to go check this out"?
It was weird because, you know when you turn on the T.V there is always the health channel there's stories on Oprah or anything like that. They talk about breast cancer, breast cancer awareness and all that stuff. Those kind of things started to appear more on TV than usual for me. I was having lunch with two of my aunts that I'm really close to, with everyone in my family. But I was having lunch with two of my aunts and they were talking about breast cancer. Someone that they know have had it. Then I mentioned that I have found a lump. It was weird because they just kind of looked at me, like when did you find it. And I have to tell them that I have been keeping it from them for a long time.

Were you scared that it might be breast cancer?
Yeah, I was. That's why I didn't say anything. I didn't want to have deal with it.

Young Sisters

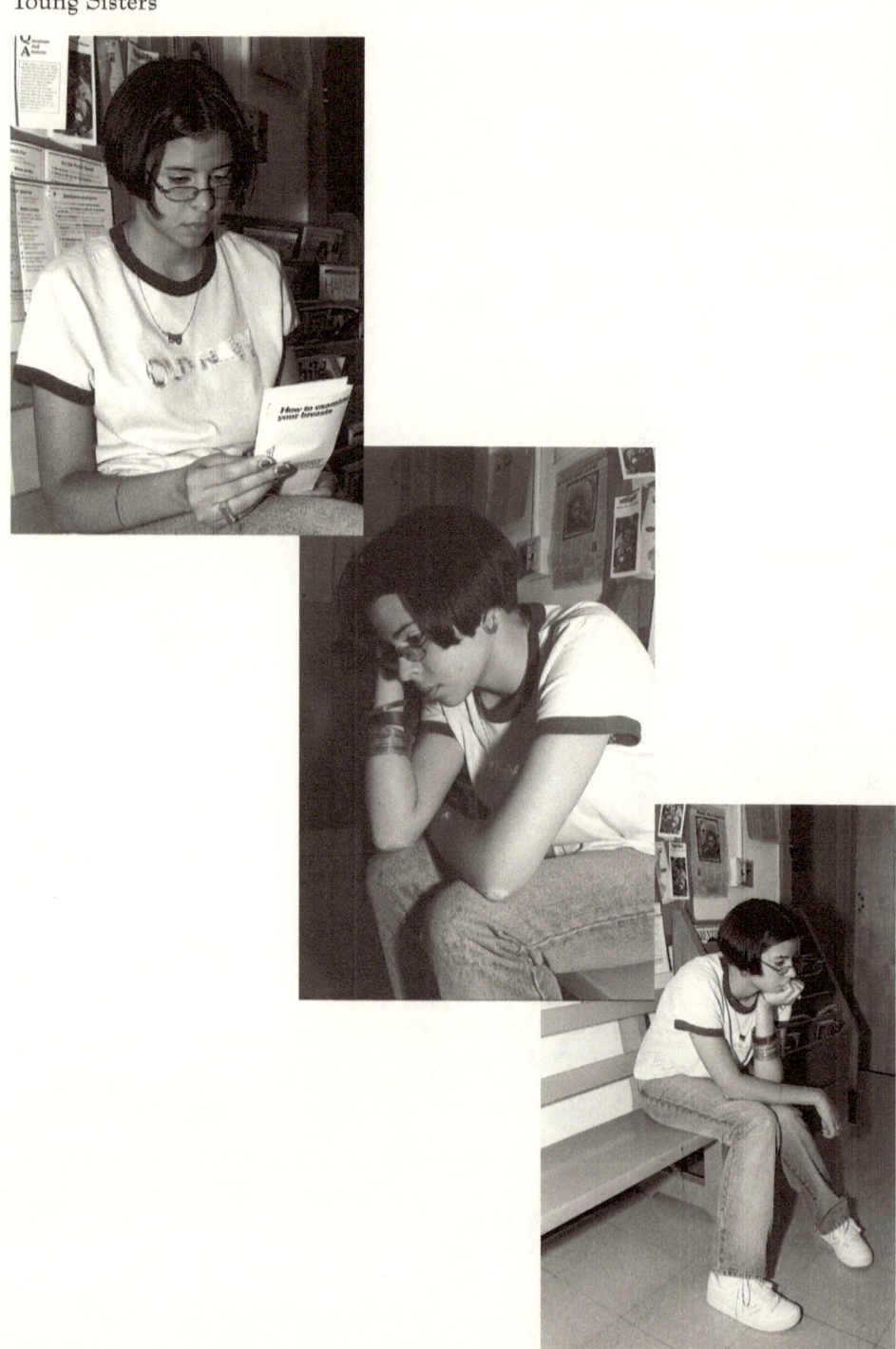

Nichole

Do any of your family members have breast cancer, because it is hereditary?
No

Now, that your aunts found out about it, did they convince you to go see a doctor?
They did convince me to go see a doctor. At the time I was living in Virginia and after living with my mother I decided to move to Virginia to kinda take a change of pace and just to see what it was like to live in a different state, different school and I got the opportunity to do that. Not because of I got problems with my mother or anything. I just wanted a change of scenery, I guest. And they decided to call my mother and talk about it and set up an appointment for me with my doctor here in New York.

We went to the doctor. He did the same check that I do on myself and saw the lump was there and said to go back in get a…not a mammogram, because I am too young to have a mammogram. I think you have to be thirty something or whatever to have a mammogram done. So I had to have a sonogram done. Like what they do on pregnant women to check to see if the baby is ok. To see inside, they put the gel on you and put the little camera on there to see. They saw the lump but we had to wait for a few more days to see what it was. Those couple of days were really nervous for me. Because I wasn't sure what it was and they don't really give you much of an idea of what anything is and I don't know much about medicine and don't know much about my body and health. It was scary, but in the end I found out that it was just something called birable nipra.

What is that?
Basically its just a mass of nothing. Its just a lump. A mass of nothing. Its not hazardous to my health. Its not cancerous or anything like that. Its not a syst, so I know some people thought it might have been that. And that's what I tried to convince myself that it was just a syst.

What's that?
Its almost like a pimple, sort of. But it is also like a mass as well. Sometimes you felt the puss that's inside of it and that can be easily remove. But it wasn't that. It was just birable nipra which is just a mass of nothing really in my breast. It was pretty large and the only thing that it could really do that would be bad for me was maybe hide another lump that might have been under it that could have been cancerous. Or it could have been a syst or be something more dangerous than this. So they still had to remove it. Which is weird, first time that I went to the doctor they told me that I had it, the doctor said we didn't need to remove it. That my breast were fibrocystic, which meant that I would probably get a lot of those. But very small like ridiculously small from the one I had. I had was maybe the size of a golf ball or maybe a little bit smaller. But he said, I didn't need to take it out, which I'm thought, "Okay, that's weird." He said that if I take it out I would have to go through more surgery and just have scars all over me. Which is weird,

because when you think about it you don't want to have scars all over your breast. So I said, "Fine lets not take it out." But he said I still need to go for follow ups like every six months to see the doctor. The next six months came and I went back and it wasn't the same doctor the doctor there had changed. And he told me that I did need to take it out and he explained to me why. Which was the reason that I just told you. That there can be something behind it, hiding anything that can be cancerous. So that was kind of nerve reckoning in itself, because I realized that I have to go through surgery and I have never gone through surgery at all in my life. I remember never staying in the hospital longer than an hour just for a check up or anything. So we decided to make an appointment two weeks after that to have the surgery. It was a pretty easy procedure. In the end, everything turnout okay. So I'm fine now. But it was scary, it was really scary thinking that I could have it. I keep on not telling anyone and keeping it to myself hoping that it would go away, but it didn't. You have to come to realization that you have to deal with what's going on.

The first doctor said you didn't need surgery and the second doctor said you should have it. What was going through your mind? Like, O my gosh, this doctor is telling you one thing and that doctor is telling you another thing. The second doctor said there might be something under it and it might be breast cancer. For you as a teenager, it must be very nerve reckoning, because you are so young and you have this disease.

It is, when I went to the second doctor, it kinda scared me when told me that, because I thought I could have been here for six months more with something that wasn't good for me. And the doctor didn't tell me anything about it. That guy didn't know what he was doing and now there is something wrong with me. So that was pretty upsetting to hear. Thinking that I was fine and I have nothing to worry about. But the second time I went they explained to me that it could be harmful to me in a certain way. So it was weird and it was upsetting. Cause as a teenager you don't want to think that you might have breast cancer.

Like I said, you watch the health channel and you watch Oprah, you see how painful it is, not just for the patient but for the family and everything to go through. Things started coming to my head like going through the treatment and everything. I didn't want to go through that. So it was pretty scary. I was really upset with the first doctor. He didn't tell me all the different things about it. He didn't really educate me on it. It was kind of hard to find things on birable nipra.

So you've done research on it?
I tried to do some, but I really didn't find much on it. Its common, but its not really dangerous and not really harmful to you. Normally, nobody really cares about it. There's not much about it. There's not much to it. There's not much to read on it.

With this whole experience, you' waited for so long to see a doctor. Have you learn anything from it? Next time when you have something small you'll go check it out.
Definitely, whether its just my breasts, whether anything on my body, my knee, my back. I know that if I have a problem I should deal with it as soon as I see that there's a problem. Cause you never know what could be wrong with you. I'm lucky that nothing is wrong with me and that I was ok. I went through a simple procedure. I was fine. Next time I might not be so lucky. But now I know if there's something wrong with me I need to go get it check out right away.

If you were go back in time when you first found it. Do you think you would go to the doctor earlier?
Most definitely. That was just eight months that I kept it to myself and not telling anyone, *not anyone* about that there could be something wrong with me. And you go through all this, things going on in your head, going through treatment, not only dealing with cancer and dying early in life, it was scary. So if I could go back and change it. I would go immediately and tell something to my family, but you can't do it again.

Do you have anything to add?
If other girls hear this and they think there's something might be wrong with them. Whether its something with their breasts or anything with their body at all. You should go check it out as soon as you find out. Tell a doctor or tell a friend if you are not comfortable with your family. If you are, tell them, I encourage you to, because you never know what's wrong with you. You could never be sure.

"Before I came to America, I felt it would be a heaven, because everybody says it. But when I came and I see everything. Right now, I feel it's the same real world."

Sabrina 16

Living Overseas

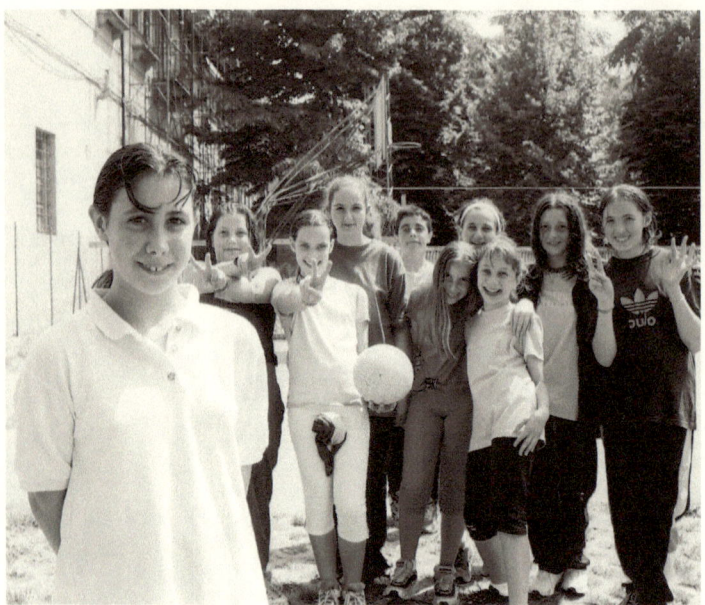

Daniela and her Italian schoolmates

Daniela 13

I'm from California, near San Francisco.

How old were you when you moved to Italy?
I was ten.

What was your reason for moving here?
That my father's Italian and he wanted to come back here.

How did you feel about it when you first have to come here?
I was really shy. I still am. (Giggles) But I would go along with my father.

Was it hard for you to adjust to come here?
Yeah, a little bit hard. Its a small language and also the culture is a bit different.

How is the culture different from here compare to California?
Well we go to school on Saturday, but we get out at 1:30.

How do you like it, here or California?
I think here is nice, because I get to experience a different country. California is also very different too.

Would you ever like to go back to California?
Maybe when I'm grown up, to go to university.

What is the best part about living in Italy?
Probably that we get off early at school. How everyday is a half day.

How is your Italian now? Are you more comfortable with the language?
A little bit.

Do you speak Italian at home or do you speak English?
We speak English. So I have to speak Italian at school.

Did you have an Italian second language course before?
No, I have to speak Italian in my Italian classes and I only speak English in
my English class.

Was it hard for you to make friends here since you didn't know the language?
Yeah.

Are they friendly here?
Yeah. I'm timid usually when I first meet people.

In California did you have interracial classes?
Yes

How is it different here?
Here, we are mostly Italians. In this school, there are about four children that
are not Italian. One girl's English, but she's in the eighth grade and another boy
who is English in the seventh grade. My brother is in the eighth grade too.

How is the teenage role here compare to America? Are there certain restrictions?
I don't think so. Is not really that different here.

Any advice for girls who are moving to another country? Suggestions?
You should be interactive with the other girls and not be...like me, I was very
timid and I didn't want to talk to anybody. But I think you should be more out
going, cause then you get to know people faster.

Would you say this is a great experience for you?
It is, because you get to experience different things. Cause I never really been out
of California before. It was a really big experience for me.

Hi! My name is Nissa   I came from Thailand. I'm 16 years old and have been here for 1 years and 7 months. My life have changed in so many ways.

First of all, my dress style changed, my hair style and my friends. My dress style had change a lot. In Thailand, we have dress code, but here we dress freely. Jeans, shorts, skirts, whatever that appropriate to the school. Then my hair style changed. At first, I will just let it goes because I don't want to have a hair cut. Now it is long, I think I will have a hair cut soon. Since none of my friends seen me with short hair before, this hair cut will surprised them!

The most things that changed in my life is friend. I wished I could go back to Thailand, I miss them so much. Here people sort of a let-it-go kind, in Thailand it is I-always-care kind. I like my Thai friends more than American friends. Even though American friends seem to be more friendly than Thai friend, I like Thai more. I like to have some people care for me, not just let it goes.

Sometimes I feel like I lost part of myself. It is Thai culture that I'm losing. From speaking, skill and writing they seem to fade away from me. I wish I could get it back soon enough.

For new teenagers that just arrive in America. I'm very grateful and welcome. It is your chance to be free and think openly. Take this chance and use your time wisely. There are many things to learn, and sometime it is just hard. Don't feel so disheartened, try your best to fight on.

Sabrina 16

How long have you been in the United States?
I think it has been around like four years and three months.

Where are you from?
China

How old were you when you moved here?
Probably like eleven to twelve.

Why did you come here?
Well it a good chance to come to another country to learn different cultures. And you have to know that in China, many people believe that America is heaven. To come here is like a fortune.

Why do people in China think coming to America is heaven?
You know America is the most powerful country in the world. They feel like if you live in America you are always so rich. Happiness. So they think its always better to come to this kind of country.

Do you feel its better to live here now?
Before I came to America, I felt it would be a heaven, because everybody says it. But when I came and I see everything. Right now, I feel it's the same real world.

What do you see that you feel is the same world?
People around are all human beings. Except for some of the building structures are very different. Other things are really the same.

Did you like living in China?
Yeah, I liked it.

What are some of the things you didn't like about living in China?
Umm, that's hard to say. Cause I came here around twelve-years-old. It has been four years, I really have like a small memory of before how did I lived. I just know that the one thing that I don't like about is the teacher give us too much homeworks. Way too much homeworks that it stress us out.

How is education different in China than in America?
Education is totally different from these two countries. In China, the teacher push you, the teachers force you to do works. They want you to be better. That's why they force you to have to finish all the homeworks. Have to do good on all the tests. In America, you have to know some of the kids, well... they don't feel education

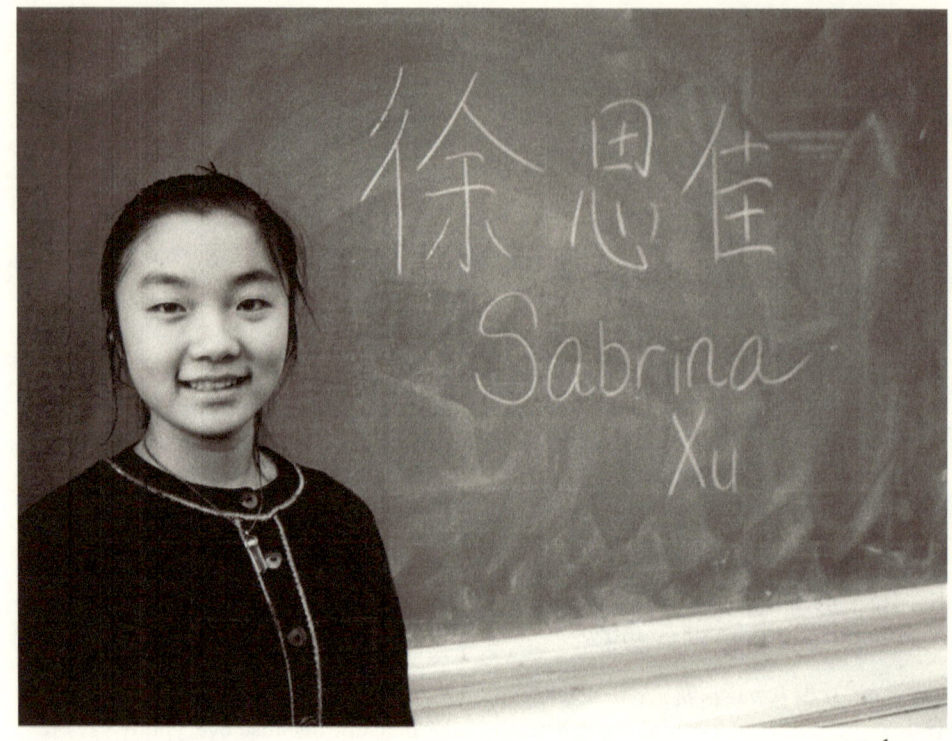

Sabrina

is really that important. And the teachers don't really mind about them. Maybe some of the teachers minds and notify or warning them, but really is not like the teachers in China where they really push you so hard. The way that America's teaching is that it depend on individuals. In China, it depends on groups. If one person out of the whole class is like the greatest, it brings glory to the whole class. America is different.

What about the female role in China compare to America?
I know that many people think that females in China are very unrightful. They don't have the right to do that, to do this. Maybe before, years and years ago like my grandmother's generation, female role is really a big difference between male. But now, to my generation, its really a slightly different, just not too much different from what the female role in America. Women go to work, take care of kids, some of the women even earn more than men. Its not like before that women cannot work, they have to stay at home, cannot go outside, take care of kids.

How many siblings do you have?
I don't have any siblings.

Is it because of China's rule that you can only have one child?
Yes, because China has too much populations during the period of Mao. Because we have too much population and the only way to decrease population is to have one family one kid. But I heard right now that the policy in China that my generation can have one or more kids.

Why is that? What is the cause for the change?
I think the policy was around 1970 something and start from that time, China's population decreased very, very great. Then the population decreased, now the older people were once so huge population is now getting older. China don't have too much to pay for the pension. Now we need population instead of we want to decrease the population. We are afraid that if we continue to have one family one kid in the future is going to be so loose. So now we are changing the policy.

How do you like living in New York? How has your life changed?
Living in New York?! Hmmm, coming to America is like the turning point of my life's history. Before I came to America, I'm really innocent, immature child like, you know. And living in China, I don't really put much effort on my education even though the teachers forces me so much. But they forces me, I don't want it. They want it. They want me to do good, not I want myself to do good.

Since I came to America, the first step that I touched America's earth, I felt everything seem so foreign to me. People speak some different languages that I don't even know and then I started learning English. And I thought learning was really fun from that time. From that matter of time, I started to push myself toward education. I think if I never get the chance to come to America or New York, I wouldn't have a bright future as I have right now. The education here is free. I get much better environment than as I lived in China.

What kind of environments are you talking about? Students or.....
Umm, well, fresh air I believe, because in China there is population, too much people squeezing on the streets. New York's environment is really better than China.

"... I'm proof that it is possible to be a student, an artist, and a human being. If you have your goals and priorities straight anything's possible."

Jessica 16

Dreams

Grace 18

I focus a lot on social issues and political issues. You try to fix things from the top. Like fix the government first. Fix society but then, you really have to fix yourself before you fix anything else. And if you fix every person one by one I think it would work so much quicker than if you try to change the system, because we make up the system.

I'm starting to get really angry at people these days, because it seems like nobody wants to do anything. Because they have so much potential. *Everyone has potential.* But they don't want to do it and they just want to hide in mediocrity.
"O let somebody else do it." Or "I don't want to be out standing." "I'll just be a normal person and that's fine for me, because its stabilize. There's no fear of failure if you don't try."

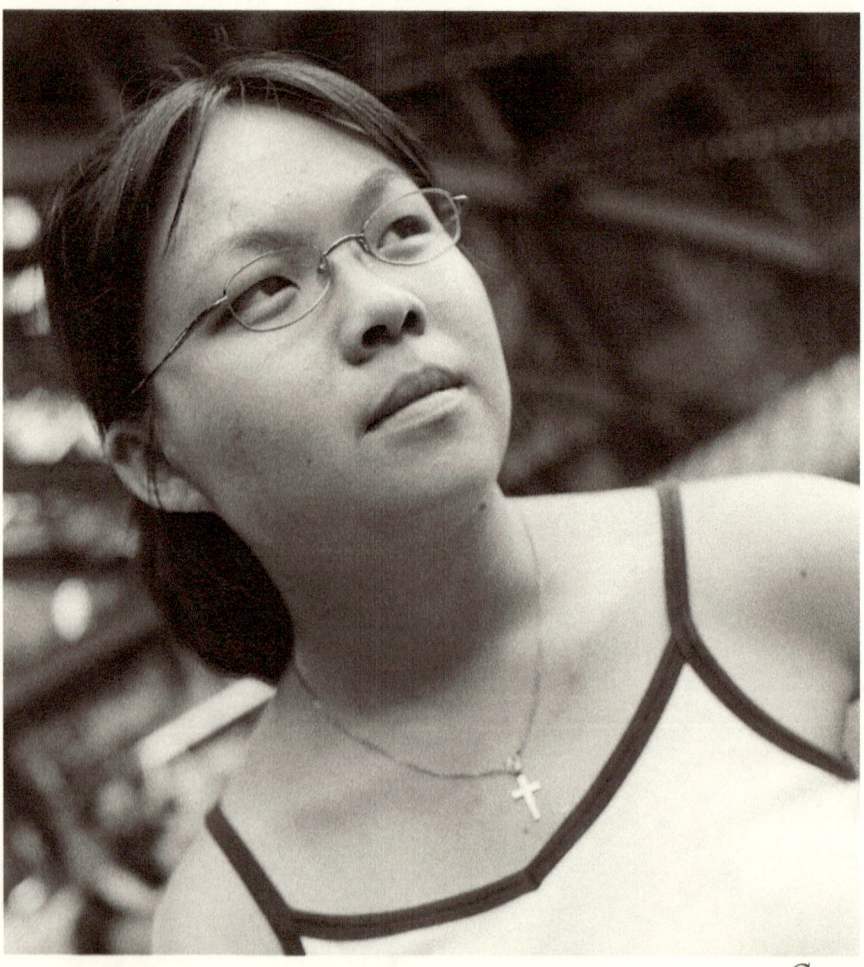

Grace

Where I work, I went to a hospital to work. It's a public hospital and my mom always tells me, "Don't work too hard. All the people will get jealous of you and they'll get mad at you and then they'll hate you and then they will conspire against you, because you're going to make them look bad."
I think that's terrible how America has turn out. I don't know how it used to be, but I think people used to work and they want to deserve what they earn. But now, everyone just want to, "I'll make money off the stock market." "I don't have to work. I don't really deserve it." No one really wants to live up to what they do anymore.

Do you think you might be like those people out there who are just like, "O, I don't want to do it, other people will take care of everything."
I don't want to do that. That is what I am afraid of doing. This goes back to Christianity. You know the parable with the talent (In Matthew 25:14-30)?
A Huh.
At first I used be to be so angry. "Hey, that's not fair. That guy, he didn't lose the money he just buried it. Why did God punished him." But now, I'm coming to realize why God punished him, because God gives each person spiritual gifts. And he might give you more than the other person, but that doesn't mean that you should hide. To bury it, is to be afraid of failure, I guest. Some people are even afraid of success, cause then they will have more responsibility. I think that's the greatest sin. You know you can do something, but you don't do it, because you are afraid of what other people might think or you are afraid you might fail.

Are you afraid of failure or success?
I'm afraid of failure.

Does that hold you back from doing things?
Yeah, that has held me back. Its like I am so focus on wanting to succeed. That sometimes I don't know what I want to succeed at. Cause I like so many things, I just want to move the world. But I don't know what I should do. I haven't really looked at myself yet and find what I really want to do or like to do. Maybe that's a problem with a lot of people that they don't know what they like.

They are still searching for it.
Yeah. But I'm trying anyway. Like, I would enter essay contest or something. Just put something on the Internet and maybe somebody would read it you know. Sometimes you get insecure too. Like what if what I write was wrong. I guest it goes back to the fear of failure.

Young Sisters

So how do you overcome these fears? Have you ever over come a fear and were actually successful in what you were doing?
I think it takes time. Like I used to be really afraid of public speaking like, *really afraid.* I would lose five pounds a week before I have to give a presentation, cause I couldn't eat. So then I got into college, so I was like, you know what I think I will join the debate team. That requires public speaking and you have to think fast. Well I wasn't really scared actually. I went to two tournaments. I did okay in one of them, but then the second one I just goofed off and did terrible. So then I got scared and I'm like, "I don't want to go back. I never want to go back." But I think just because I said I never want to go back, I should go back. I probably will.

That's good, that's like overcoming your fears.
Yeah

And its like you said, it takes time. Step by step.
Yeah just let yourself go. Like acting. Cause you know I was really shy. I didn't want to act or anything. But, my art teacher, he was in theater. He was in charge of this play. He was like, "Why don't you just join. I'll give you a small part." And then I realized that once I let myself go, you think, "O, its not so bad." You just flow with it. You feel like really happy being yourself and doing what you want to do and not be afraid. It's the first step that is the hardest. Just one day dress differently, you know. Like say something. Just raise your hand in class and say something. You realize, hey its not so bad.

So just take chances and not be inhibit in doing things?
Especially when you think you don't have the ability. I mean everybody has the ability. If you say this is the best I can do, its not. There is no such thing as the best.

So push yourself harder to go to the next level.
Yeah.

Gloria

17 yrs. old

It took me 3 times before I won
Miss NY Teen USA. The 1st yr. I was
the 3rd runner-up, the next yr. I
was the 1st runner-up. This yr.
I won the title, I put the pressure
on myself to win, I knew I couldn't
go anywhere but up.

My preparation for Miss Teen USA
is your basic working out, not to
lose weight, but to tone up my
body. Of course my favorite part, the
shopping for wardrobe for all the types
of events at Miss Teen USA. And I
was provided 2 coaches, 1 for hair,
make-up, walking and wardrobe,
and the other to help me on my interview
and communication skills for the
interview part at Miss Teen USA.

I started competing because I always
watched Miss Teen USA on TV And I
always dreamed of competing for it. When
I saw my idol, Vanessa Minillo win in 1998
I wanted to be just like her. She was a
natural, beautiful girl and she did such an
awesome job during her reign as Miss Teen USA
and she was a great spokesperson for DARE
which is the Miss Teen USA platform.

The best part of the pageant is
meeting all the girls. The worst part is
waking up early to rehearse.

To me competitions as big as
the one I won is not unfair. I would

say it anything it is extremely fair. They do (the judges) their job in picking who they feel will do the best job in representing the state (NY) at Miss Teen USA.

Pageants dont expose girls to be pretty and skinny. Pageants to me give girls self-confidence and are a good experience.

My advice to girls who want to join pageants is do it because you want to. Go in with an open mind, be prepared to lose or win. make friends at the pageants because friends last longer than a sash, crown, and title.

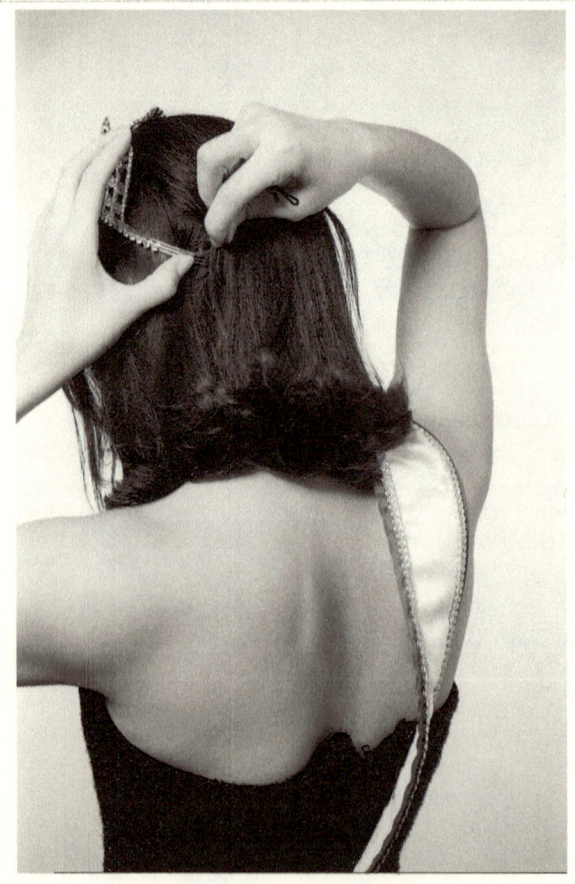

As Miss New York Teen USA 2001, I spent most of my year doing appearances and volunteering.

I volunteered for both the Breast Cancer and Aids walk in NYC. I signed in participants, and collected donations. I of course also walked with celebrities like RuPaul, Erik McCormack of Will & Grace, Jillian Parry Miss Teen USA 2000 and Denise Quiñones, Miss Universe 2001.

On the weekends I would spend my time at an elderly center in my hometown of The Bronx. The Maria Isabel Center. I would serve food, sign autographs, and spend time talking to each person.

I also did many appearances, as the first Latina to win Miss New York Teen USA, I appeared in Latingirl magazine, the Puerto Rican Day Parade, and I judged special events, ex. talent shows, other local pageants, etc.
I also appeared in a fashion show for designer Nime Jamal.

→

My favorite appearances would
have to be cutting the ribbon
at new Burger king
openings. I posed for pictures,
signed autographs, spoke to
children about becoming Miss
New York Teen USA (2001), how
to stay in school, follow
their dreams etc. I also
had the opportunity of calling
up a few random people
telling them they were the
winner of a brand new
mountain bike, courtesy of
Burger king. Hearing their
voices, when I told them who
I was and what they had
won, will always be something
special I will never forget.

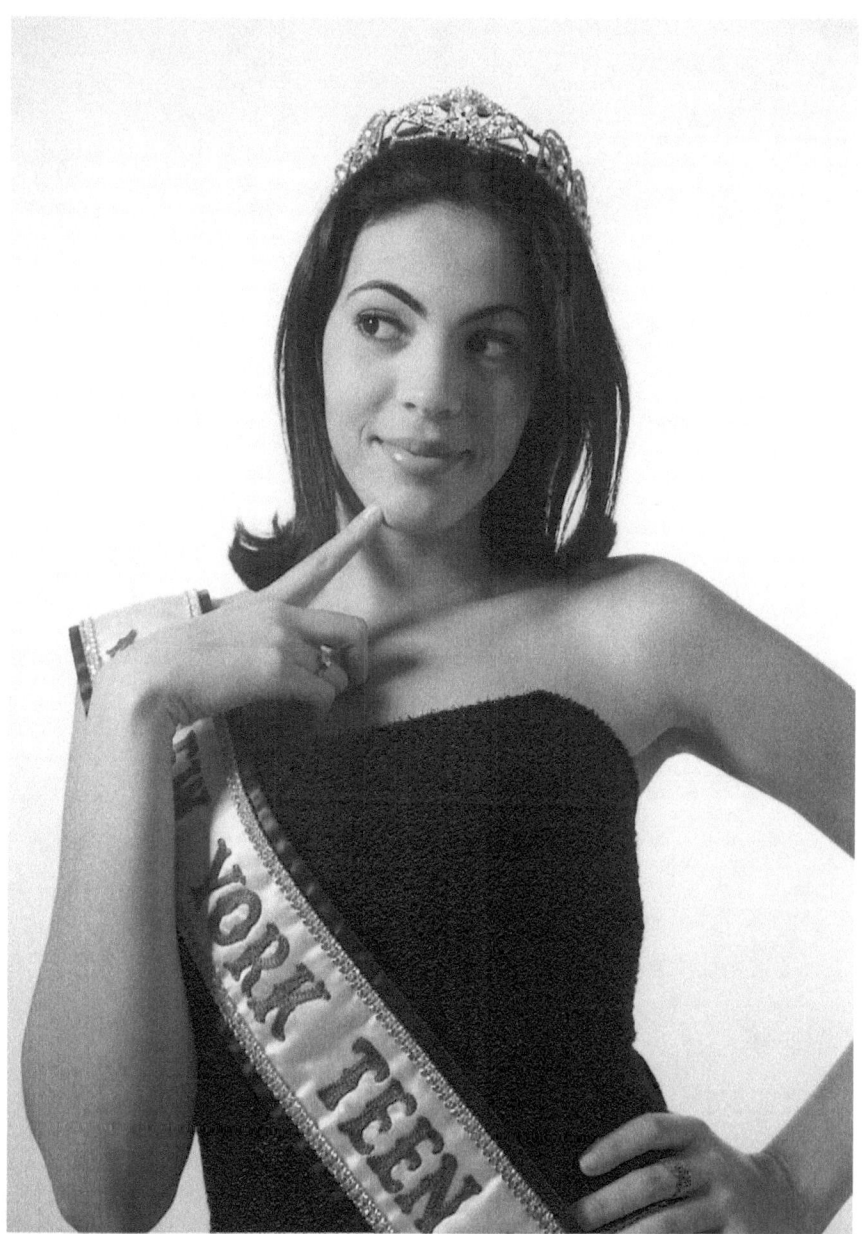

Gloria

I have a dream .... about Basketball
I'm Casandra   I have this dream about getting a college scholarship to a good basketball college (like Duke or UConn) and then go to the WNBA. I've had this dream since I was 8 but I first picked up a ball when I was 3. I kept playing basketball up til' now. I have the best coach in N.Y. Coach Nelson (Tom Nelson) has been coaching me for 3 years now. I'm also on his traveling team called the "Spangles." We have gone to tournants in Pennsylvania, Utica, and more. The thing is that we live in Rome, NY and we keep traveling until we win all those games

Basketball is one thing that keeps me in school. Without it, I think I would be a mess. Basketball is a goal that I can look forward to. I think my coach can help me toward my goal. He has done so much for me already and can do so much more. If it weren't for him and my mom (him for coaching, my mom for support), I wouldn't have made the basketball for modified without him. Thanks to Coach Nelson, I can work more on my basketball career.

Now when I go to college, I want to be

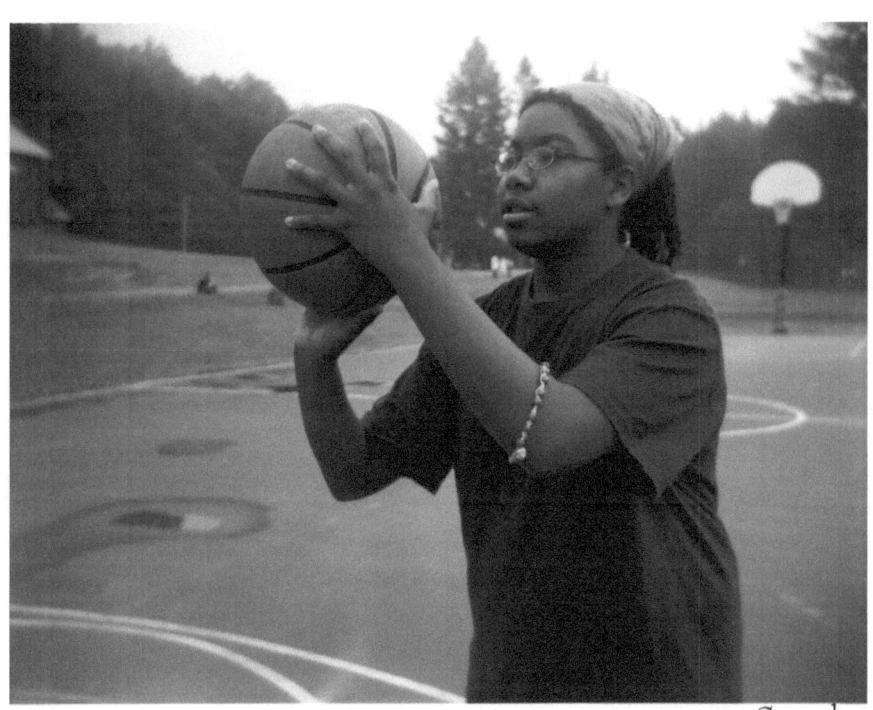

Casandra

Seen by a coach for WNBA. My favorite teams are Liberty, Sparks, and Comets. My favorite player/basketball role model is Cynthia Cooper. She lived a tough **childhood** and during and after that, she worked on her basketball skills. Later she made it to the WNBA and stayed for quite some time. Then, she retired and became a coach for the WNBA teams. Cooper lived a good life (at least in the end). I always wanted to be her, maybe someday I will but I have to take it one step at a time. All I need is to practice, practice and practice.

Basketball does another thing, relieves peer pressure and stress. The thing is I want to stay healthy for basketball. Basketball is the reason I won't do drugs or sex. It's one of my anti-drugs. Whenever I get stressed, I'll go outside and shoot hoops. I'm proud of my talent and I will pursue my dream.

Leonella

I, Leonella was born to (two) wonderful couple Bertille and Morretta on the 13th May 1986.

I grew in a beautiful home until at the age of eight (8) my family broke up. My mom was against my uncle (dad's brother) living with us, so she asked my dad to put my uncle out, since my dad didnot agree, she put it herself to leave. She left us in 1995, my sister Sevina was four (4), my brother was six (6) and my dad.

I'll being the eldest had to do all the chores in the house, wash dishes, cook, do laundry to name a few. It was hard for me since I had to keep up with school and my dad had to work. My mom visited us at times but it was always painful to see her leave. Couple of years later with all the struggle and heart break I got into high school with good grades. Then my mom wrote us (and said) saying that she was pregnant I was horrified, since I still had hopes that her dyparture was only temporary and she would come back and the family would reconcile. High school was even more struggle since the village I'm living in, is small and everyone just wanted me to fall. They all look down upon me, to talk and condemn, the minute if I stps out of line. All my friends from the same village that went to school with me dropped out dew to pregnancies, finances etc I was the only student from my village to go right through high school until the end. Then right to the end of high school I received another letter from my mom, again she was pregnant, I began to cry then, it was right before my final exams to get out of high school, it shook me up so much I could not concentrate on my school work, but miraculously I passed my exams. Presently I'm teaching for the time being and aspiring to be a lawyer one day.

My name is Jessica Danser. Every day after school and on Saturdays I study dance at the Ailey school. I take technique classes in ballet and modern and I learn repertory pieces to perform. On Saturday mornings I help teach younger girls - these are my work hours for my scholarship. Since I passed an audition, I don't have to pay to dance, but I do work (teaching) every week instead.

My grades in school are pretty high, my average is about a 95. It's hard to have any kind of a social life when I'm so busy, but I have friends in school + at dance, so it's not like I have no social contact. I usually manage to talk on the phone just about every night + some Saturday nights I go out if I'm not too exhausted. If I had a choice between dance + a social life, dance would definitely win. It's my greatest joy in life. It's everything to me.

I don't really consider myself a role model for other teenagers. I accomplish everything I do because I want to and because I'm just naturally efficient. I guess if anything, I'm proof that it is possible to be a student, an artist, and a human being. If you have your goals + priorities straight anything's possible.

J Danser

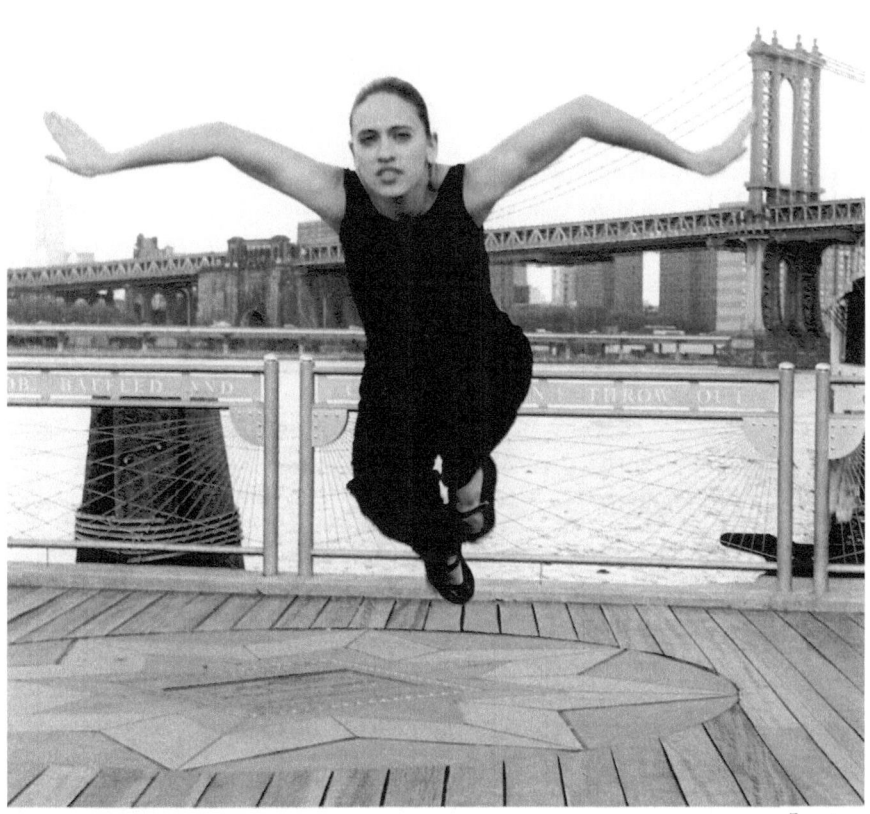

Jessica

Hotlines
Key:
24/7 - 24 hours a day, 7 days a week
PCT - Pacific Coast Time
ET - Eastern Time

General
Covenant House Nine Line
1800 999-9999
24/7
Crisis line for youth and parents.
Referrals throughout the US.

Focus Adolescent Services
http://www.focusas.com
Deals with a variety of teen issues with
information, resources, and support.

Teen Line
www.teenlineonline.org
Teenage yellow pages
1800 852-8336
Mon-Sun 6pm-10pm PCT
Teen to teen counseling.

Youth Crisis Hotline
1800 843-5200
1800 448-4663
24/7. Bilingual (Spanish).
For parents and youth in crisis.

Abuse
Child Abuse Hotline
1800 540-4000
Available in Spanish.
To report abuse.

Child help USA National Child Abuse
1800 422-4453
Crisis intervention for child abuse.

Info Link National Center for Victims
of Crime
1800 394-2255
TTY 1800 211-7996
Mon-Fri 5:30am-5:30pm
Referrals nationwide.

AIDS
Center for Disease Control
1800 342-2437
1800 344-7432 Spanish
Information, support, referrals.

Alcohol
Alcohol & Drug Helpline
1800 821-4357

Alcoholics Anonymous
www.alcoholics-anonymous.org

National Clearance for Alcohol and
Drug Information
1800 662-HELP

For friends and family of someone
with drinking problems
1800 344-2666

National Drug and Alcohol Treatment
1800 662-HELP
24/7. Available in Spanish.
The staff are trained counselors and
have referral service for local
treatment options.

Crisis
California Youth Crisis Line
1800 843-5200
All problems. Spanish language
available.

Hit Home Youth Crisis Line
1800 448-4663
Referral hotline for youth in crisis.

Counseling
Child Help USA
1800 422-4453
24/7
Telephone counseling and referrals.

Gamblers Anonymous
1800 448-3000

Girls and Boys Town National
Hotline
www.boystown.org
1800 448-3000

National Child Abuse Hotline
1800 422-4453
24/7
Crisis intervention information

National Domestic Violence
1800 799-SAFE
TTY 1800 787-3224
For local resources and confidential
counseling.

National Youth Violence Prevention
Resource Center
www.safeyouth.org
1866 SAFEYOUTH
1866 723-3968
1888 503-3952 (TTY)
8am to 6pm ET
Deals with psychological, emotional,
physical, and sexual abuses.
The resource is for professionals,
parents, and youths working to
prevent violence committed by and
against young people.

Rape Abuse and Incest National
Network (RAINN)
www.rainn.org
1800 656-HOPE
24/7
For survivors of sexual assault.
Call for support and counseling.

National Sexual Assault Hotline
1800 656-HOPE
24/7. Confidential.

Victims of Crime Resource Center
1800 842-8467
Mon – Fri 8am- 6pm

Drugs
California's Smokers Helpline
www.nobutts.ucsd.edu
1800 662-8887
Mon-Fri 9am-9pm
Sat 8am-1pm

Cocaine and Heroin Hotline
www.drughelp.org
1800 622-HELP

Drug – Alcohol Helpline
1800 821-4357

Narcotics Anonymous
www.na.org

National Drug and Alcohol Treatment
1800 662-HELP (1800 662-4357)
24/7. Available in Spanish.
Provides information on drug and
alcohol abuse. The staff are trained
counselors and have referral service for
local treatment options.

Relapse Prevention Hotline
1800 662-4357

Eating Disorders and Depression
1800 339-6993
General information and referrals.

Bulimia / Anorexia Self Help Hotline
1800 448-3000

Eating Disorder Recovery Online
www.edrecovery.com

Eating Disorders Awareness and
Prevention (EDAP)
www.edap.org
1800 931-2237

National Mental Health Association
Helpline
1800 969-6642

United Way Crisis Help line
1800 233-4357

GED
1800 626-9433
24/7. Learn how to take a GED.

Homework
1800 527-8839
24/7. Closed during summer

Human Trafficking
1888 3737-888
Trafficking Information and referrals
24/7

Pregnancy
Emergency Contraception Hotline
1800 584 -9911

Family Planning Referral Hotline
1800 942-1054

Rape
Asian Rape Crisis Hotline (Includes
domestic violence)
1800 339-3940
24/7. Asian languages spoken.
Counseling and finding a shelter.

Rape Abuse and Incest National
Network (RAINN)
www.rainn.org
1800 656-HOPE
24/7. Spanish avaliable. Confidential.
For survivors of sexual assault. Call
for support and counseling. Referrals,
information, and resources available.

Runaway
Children of the Night
www.childrenofthenight.com
1800 551-1300
24/7. Spanish,
Russian (Mon-Fri 9-5pm)
Referrals available.
Shelters for runaways, prostitutes,
11-17 years old.

National Runaway Switchboard
www.1800runaway.org
1800 621-4000
1 800 RUNAWAYS
24/7. Translation to other
languages available.
For parents and youth in crisis.
Offers crisis counseling and information
referral. Provides information about
various programs for runaways, such as
free bus rides home, shelter, etc.

Missing Children Hotline
www.caag.state.ca.us/missing
1800 222-3463
24/7. Interpreter available.

Sexual Transmitted Disease
National STD Hotline
www.drughelp.org
1800 227-8922
Mon-Fri 5am-8pm

Suicide
1800-SUICIDE (1800 784-2433)
24/7. Other languages are available.
Trained volunteers and professional
counselors ready to listen.
Information and referrals available.

Yellow Ribbon Project
www.yellowribbon.org
Help prevent teen suicide

Everyone has a choice to love or hate. We all possess the power to build each other up or tear one another down. What is your choice? I choose to love and it has become a passion that instills a hunger in me to serve victims of oppression and poverty, and especially victims of human trafficking. This is my purpose and mission in life. Social destruction does not have to occur if we just take some time and reflect on how we can make someone's life better everyday. Society can be a much better place. My life is a living testimony to that statement. My family, friends, and mentors have taken time out to guide me through life with encouragement, constructive criticism, and love. There is a chain here: positive people and positive relationships produce excellent fruits. I hope this book will touch you and help you connect with a new sense of how to deepen your life. Most of all, I want to encourage you to give back to society with your time and resources.

I would like to hear from you. Please send your comments about this book to me in the e-mail below. Thank you.

info@AnnaLeung.org

Please visit my website for more products and services on *Young Sisters*

www.AnnaLeung.org

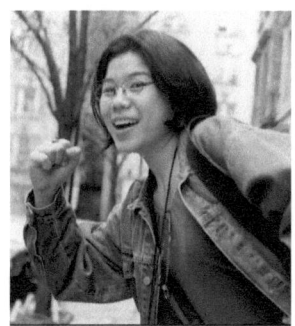

About the Author

Anna Leung started photography at twelve-years-old. By fourteen, she interned at Fashion Institute of Technology (FIT) as a teacher's assistant for professor Curtis Willocks. For three years, her responsibilities included setting up the studio before class and teaching college and adult students *Photo 101*. At sixteen, her photographic documentary on New York City's diminishing meatpacking district was displayed in the Noho gallery and *Around the Way* magazine. At seventeen, she won The American Theater Wing's playwriting contest. Turning nineteen, she received second prize in a photo contest that was published in Rochester Institute of Technology's *Signatures Magazine*. Throughout college Anna enthusiastically volunteered for overseas mission trips every spring break assisting projects such as building a ropes course, spending time at an orphanage, and transforming a dumpsite into a playground to name a few. She also studied in Spain for a semester and completed her public policy bachelor's degree in three years at Rochester Institute of Technology (RIT).

Anna Leung wants to inspire, encourage, and motivate people to be productive citizens who continuously benefit society by planting seeds of **hope**. She finds joy in serving others, especially those who are victims of human trafficking. She believes evil and suffering exist because good people are standing on the sidelines being apathetic. She knows if we all work together as a team to help fix ourselves and society then great feats can be accomplished.

www.ingramcontent.com/pod-product-compliance
Lightning Source LLC
Chambersburg PA
CBHW020433290526
45785CB00002B/835